SHAWNDA CHRISTIANSEN

Miles To Go

On Broken Wings

MEGA REEL
ENTERTAINMENT

This book was professionally typeset on Reedsy.
Find out more at reedsy.com

This book is dedicated, to everyone who slammed a door,
everyone who opened a door,
all of the films cast, crew,
and chickens.
Stay tuned, "JUNKIE" the film, book series, sequel, et al,
will be taking over the world momentarily.
Thank you for fueling the inspiration to shine a light in dark places.
(HUGS)
We've got miles to go.

"Sometimes the best moments in life are found in the simplest of things, slipping away over time to be replaced by the horrors of senseless cruelties…"

Contents

Foreword

This is a new edition to the previously published book *Junkie – Broken Wings* re-edited with additional chapters.

When I sat down to add some stuff to this book and republish it under its new name, a lot had changed in my life including the loss my father. It still feels like he died yesterday although it has been much longer than that, and it was because of his death that I learned a lesson I could not have learned any other way.

Mortality.

We all know that we will die someday but we don't truly understand the gravity of our own mortality until we have lost someone that has been our pillar of strength for 50 years. My stepmother had died 12 years earlier, while it was surreal it was not the same as when my father died.

Learning more about my own mortality has changed my life in many ways and inspired me to add an additional chapter about that as well. Anyone can change course at any point in their lives, miracles do happen, and if you desire change in your life – take that first step today.

In this new edition, you will find twelve additional chapters. Adding these additional chapters helped me close numerous chapters of my past so that I will be better prepared for the new chapters that await me.

Thank you very much for joining me on this journey and I hope you will join me on my next journey. My first supernatural book is in progress right now, The Slayer Chronicles – Volume I – it's going to be a lot of fun. See you there.

Preface

Letter from the author

I had quite a few years clean and was working as a Substance Abuse counselor when I first set out to write this book. I must admit that I was hesitant to share a lot of the personal details of my story, and some of them are being shared for the very first time – in the coming chapters. It took me a lot of years to get here, it seemed every time I began to write I would just stop. When I returned to continue writing, I deleted everything and started over.

This was the way the book started and continued for years until one day I decided that the story would be told best as a television series – which was probably just another excuse to delay the book but I wrote the pilot episode and titled the series: JUNKIE. The title was an honest accident, I just needed to save my work and had to give it a name. I had originally planned to name the book: "I Never Said I Wanted to be a Junkie When I Grew Up." So, it just made sense to temporarily save the screenplay as: "JUNKIE."

I felt strongly that in order to maintain my focus on the pitch pilot I needed to create some artwork. I played around for a while with sketches and wanted a depiction of the moment of clarity that got me clean (the moment in my addiction when I finally knew I was crazy). I decided to contact my photographer friend, I told her what I wanted to capture and she immediately invited me over.

We captured the bathtub suicide attempt. It was a brutal, unadulterated depiction of my moment of clarity, the propulsion that facilitated the change in my life. It was my first personal announcement that I was coming to the film industry, and I would be telling the brutal, honest story of what addiction can lead to.

The photos were shared on social media and were met with a wave of negative responses because they looked like someone had taken photos of a young woman who had just cut her wrists in the bathtub. There were knock down drag out social media fights going on about suicide not being something to joke about. Then suddenly there was a Facebook page "JUNKIE" and all of the shocking photos were on there. I had no idea how the page or the name surfaced on social media until later, when I learned that someone had peeked at the screenplay, then created the page for it. By then we had already shocked so many people with the imagery and name that I would have been shooting my project in the foot if I changed it – so it stayed. We picked up a lot of followers overnight due to the negative publicity we received, it was an awkward way to start out but at least we were reaching people.

Over time the series concept continued to develop as I was pounding out the entire first season with my writing team. I had my ear to the ground and was learning everything I could about film production when I learned the difference between distributing a series vs distributing a feature film. It is rare for a first-time filmmaker to succeed at a series from a mere promo reel or pitch pilot. The entire first season should be shot to ensure optimal results, but it isn't as rare for a first-time filmmaker to get distribution for a feature film, as long as the film is strong. The stronger the film, the greater the distribution possibilities are.

It was really important to me to make sure that my story reached as many people as possible. It seemed like the smartest business move was to produce a feature film first, with the series to follow. So, I discussed my thoughts with my director, who agreed that it was the smartest move in front of us. He helped turn the pilot episode into a beat sheet for a feature length film. Next we just had to write our screenplay.

It was important to me to write the first draft of the screenplay, because there were elements from my personal story that I wanted to ensure were a part of the film. So, I sat down and did just that. Other members of the writing team took passes at it as well and our end result was very much a group effort. I finally produced the film JUNKIE: Miles to go with the help of a lot of wonderful people who believed in the message of the story and wanted to see it come to life. It was nothing short of a truly amazing accomplishment and thanks to the flawless dynamics of our cast and crew, JUNKIE the film has Miles to go.

The process of that achievement and the people I met along the way finally gave me the courage to finish this brutally honest book. People don't see the need to change until the pain of the present becomes too unbearable to carry on. That's what hitting bottom is, it is when the pain is finally too much. The great thing about bottom is that the only way left to go is up.

This novel tells the detailed, brutally honest story of how I spiraled down to the bottom. The pits of hell, and thanks to a miracle, or I guess I should say a few miracles I was suddenly lifted out of the pits. It is my hope that anyone who reads this will see that there is always hope for change, regardless of the type of hole we have buried ourselves in: addiction, abusive relationships, financial turmoil – there is always the possibility for change so long as we are still alive.

In order to accomplish my goals with this novel, I have to be as brutally honest about my past as I can be. I have protected the innocent, so any depictions of real life experiences that involved other people have been altered for that purpose. June Taylor's experiences are all true as she walks you down the dark roads of the brutal truth of being a rock bottom junkie. Yet, no matter how far she spirals: sexual assaults, suicide attempts, needle obsessions, hallucinations, ghosts, a love affair with methamphetamine, she still manages rise up from the ashes of hell and become a new woman - proving that anything is possible.

Acknowledgement

Jack Henslee. A hero, a father, a veteran, a savior to thousands of men and women who have lost their voices. A savior to me, on my journey to hell and back. It's doubtful I would be here without him. I don't mention him in my story with exception of a quote from his beautiful poem about surviving Cancer. Our relationship is a special one that I chose to keep to myself. Author of the book "Look Who's Talking" and poem *The Sounds of Silence*, mentor to thousands of men and women who have lost their voices to cancer. They call him a hero. I get to call him daddy. Thanks for everything Dad, you're amazing.

I miss you. I have never in my life, known what I would do if I lost you. You were always my rock, my pillar, the one person in this world that cared when it was my birthday. I will never forget all of the years I was out wandering the world, in a really bad place, you always sent me a birthday card with cash in it. Sometimes, I would be so high that I would have forgotten it was my birthday, till a card showed up in the mail.

Over the years of my life I had grown accustomed to receiving from you but never giving. I think that my years of addiction played a huge role in that, as if I conditioned myself to just count on you – never really thinking of the fact that you might like to count on me too.

One day I realized that when I suddenly realized I didn't know when your birthday was and never sent you anything for Father's Day. I am ashamed of how old I actually was, and how far along into my recovery I was, when I came to realize that.

I thank God every day that I moved closer to you and was able to be there for you during the last few years of your life. I worry every day I'm going to get myself into a mess that I can't get out of, and not have you there to lean on.

I know it is selfish of me, because you have moved onto your new plain of existence. Death is not the end; it is the beginning. You have visited my dreams enough to make sure I always remember that. I have added an additional section to this book, to share all of that for you, for me, and for anyone who reads this book.

You, the Reader. This book is dedicated to you for taking the time to read the story of another person who went to hell, turned around, and came back. I hope that you read this all the way to the end, I was crying when I wrote the final chapters. The tears were from a place of deepest gratitude for the love and understanding I was shown by complete strangers. There is love in this world, in the hearts of everyone around us, just waiting to be set free.

Tim Russ. I also want to thank Tim Russ for helping mold my series concept into a feature length film. It is because of him that it is a compelling story that shows the transformation of a woman from being a rock bottom junkie with absolutely no hope for change. Then her metamorphosis into a beautiful and strong woman who can do anything. The way he depicted the transformation of a phoenix rising from the ashes is nothing short of breathtaking and those who watch the film are truly moved by her transformation.

Anna Easteden. Tim laid the groundwork but then it was up to the actress Anna Easteden to deliver the character. She is absolutely monumental in her performance. She has a light Finnish accent that I came to love for my character because during my days as a rock bottom junkie I didn't sleep a lot and several people said I talked like I had a soft Norwegian accent (due to the sleep deprivation). Occasionally, I hear Anna's soft subtle accent in her performance as June Taylor and it truly nails the role from a very personal place for me.

Christian Kane. I also need to express my deepest gratitude to the actor Christian Kane. I was familiar with Christian Kane from his role in a TV series called Angel. It's funny because a couple of years after I finally got my head off the drugs and had a place of my own a new TV show began titled "Buffy the Vampire Slayer." I absolutely loved that show. The female lead goes through quite the transformation as well. I often associated her as a person who finds a way to rise above her oppressors – even when it seems impossible. When you subtract the supernatural element, you see that is really what the show is about and that is why it works so well.

When they split off and began the show Angel, I followed with the rest of the crowd and that is where I first saw Christian Kane. I never finished watching the series, life kind of does that sometimes. Then just two years before I began production on the film, a friend pointed out to me that in the final seasons of that show my favorite Buffy character Spike joins it in a big way. So, I sat down and watched the final two seasons and Christian Kane's character actually won me over, becoming my favorite.

Fast forward two years to the production of the feature film, Junkie. I was contacted by an individual who stated he knew some talent and he could help me out with my film. I told him I was seeking an actor for Sheriff Corbin. He kept sending me lists of names and occasionally he'd say he could get me Christian Kane. I didn't realize who he was talking about and once he even asked if I saw his message, as he was really surprised I didn't respond.

My co-producer Jason was a huge Leverage fan. One day while he was watching it he paused it and said, "Look at the TV, wouldn't it be nice to get this guy as the Sheriff?" I looked at the TV and said, "Hey! That's the corrupt lawyer from Angel, love him but how in the world would we ever get that guy?" Jason suggested that we locate his agent, so I said, "I'll try, what's his name?" Jason said, "That's Christian Kane."

I felt like the stupidest person in the world as I looked back through my email thread and confirmed his name was on the list of potential talent, then immediately replied, "If it's not too late, please send the screenplay out to Christian, we need to get him, as fast as we can." I was worried we had taken too long, as we were getting really close to our start date, but it all worked out.

I am unbelievably grateful to have had Christian Kane in this film. He delivers an absolute powerhouse performance. It is hard to describe how perfect his performance is but everyone who has seen the film walks away from it absolutely blown away with Christian Kane's "wow" performance. He is the embodiment of the character, through and through. I am truly blessed to have had one of my favorite actors, from one of my favorite shows in my feature film debut. It was also a true joy to have him on set as he eased the minds and insecurities of the local performers that were intimated to work around such a seasoned professional. Several of the local performers raved about how Christian Kane put their nerves at ease and guided them on set.

The Kaniacs. His fans the "Kaniacs" are also an amazing group of women who have shown me and the entire film team nothing but love and support throughout this entire process. These women are a worldwide force of love and support. I have been fortunate to call them a part of the JUNKIE family and even though they only love us because of Christian Kane, it is love, it is pure, and they will forever be in my heart.

So, thank you Tim Russ, and Christian Kane for helping me succeed with my feature film debut. You have helped carry my story to a lot of people, which is monumental. I also want to thank the Kaniacs for helping us spread the word worldwide, and every single person who played a part in the production of JUNKIE, thank you Jason Knittle, Matt Hunt, Ryan Betzler and Wendy Nelson for believing in the story as much as I did – you are a large part of the reason I was able to complete this film.

Film cast and crew. It takes a village to make a feature film, I want to thank every single member of that village from start to finish.

Jason Knittle. Thank you, Jason, for everything, from getting the commitment from Tim Russ all the way through the never-ending post production needs and expenses.

Matt Hunt. I also want to thank Matt Hunt for all of the love and ongoing support from start to finish. Not just with the film but with the book and all of my other projects, too. Matt Hunt has become a true and dear friend who has enriched my life in more ways than one.

Stacey Banks. I met Stacey on the set of JUNKIE. We began talking afterwards, mostly about school and my son. She ultimately ended up helping me with the initial outline of this novel, and I am forever grateful to her for it. She truly has a heart of gold.

Robin Penninger. Her beautiful eye for art helped me bring my stories to life with an amazing book cover.

Wendy Nelson. She slid in at the end as the true novel hero and rescued me from the perpetual hell of revisions with the soundest advice I have ever been given.

Seth Mason. My son, who keeps me hopeful about my future, always reminding me of why I need to strive every day to be a better person.

Butterfly

A young girl runs up a driveway and almost steps on a Monarch butterfly. She pauses, kneels down and watches as it struggles to free itself from the water. One wing is stuck to the cement like glue, as the free wing flaps furiously and its little legs struggle to gain leverage.

She watches for a long time, admiring all of the beautiful colors. Then she stands back up, runs into the house, runs all the way into her room and dumps out a shoe box. She runs back to the butterfly and grabs it. Gently pulling if from the pavement, she finally manages to get it and gently places it inside of the box.

She looks around and sees another butterfly feeding from a flower. She runs over to the flower bush and plucks several flowers from the bush then places those into the box and runs back into her room. She places the box in her closet then runs to the kitchen.

She returns with a bowl of water and places that in the box too. She tends to the needs of the butterfly.

Each day when she comes home from school she brings the butterfly fresh flowers. Her and the butterfly begin an exercise. She holds the flower in front of the butterfly, low, and the butterfly tries to fly to the flower. It's difficult at first as the butterfly's flutter is akin to a person with a cast on their leg, but each day the butterfly does better.

Eventually the butterfly goes into full flight to the flower, then flies onto the little girl's hand. The butterfly crawls all over the giggling and happy little girl. She is proud of what she has accomplished.

She opens her curtain to let the butterfly take off into the world. The butterfly somehow understands her as they have developed a communication entirely of their own. It takes flight.

Sadly, she had not opened the window yet, so the butterfly hits the glass really hard and falls down.

Concerned, she places her hand in front of the stunned butterfly and smiles as he crawls up onto her finger.

If butterflies can get embarrassed this one certainly was.

She opened the window, the butterfly waited as she popped out the screen.

She held the butterfly up to the open window, but the butterfly hesitated.

A breeze welcomed the butterfly, bringing with it an inherent feeling of safety.
The butterfly took flight, out through the window.
She sat down on her bed, a little sad her friend was gone.
The butterfly flew back in, landed on her nose for a moment, and flew away.
The butterfly was gone but the relationship between them was something that
would last forever.

One

The Beginning of The End

⤖

S ometimes to truly appreciate life's lessons we have to look deeper.
A lot deeper.
And look both ways before we cross the street.

A 1970's style sprinkler-swooshes across a grassy terrain on a beautiful summer day as a little girl runs through the stream of water, skipping over the dandelions with a big beautiful smile on her face. Sometimes the best moments in life are found in the simplest of things – slipping away over time to be replaced by the horrors of senseless cruelties. Not this day though, this is a day for grabbing onto the purest of joys.

The little girl picks a dandelion and blows the florets into the breeze as she runs towards a door. The door opens and an adult June Taylor steps through, a transparent apparition of the little girl passes through her in the doorway. June has no recollection of a time in her life when she felt the mere urge to smile. Those memories have been swallowed whole by something larger: apathy, darkness and despair.

June stands at the threshold, duffle bag in hand as she scans the room, asking herself how she got so far into the darkness. Maybe it was the abuse, or maybe the empty relationships, or maybe it was the drugs?

She passes by a pool table on the right-hand side and a bar on the left.

June is shaking as she sets her duffle bag down on the floor. She places a hand over her stomach to settle the butterflies.

She looks down the corridor and sees what appears to be an office; an elderly woman spots June through the office window and stands up.

Janet Trump waddles out of the office door the way some elderly women do, and makes her way down the corridor towards June, sizing her up from head to toe with a certain scrutiny, the way some elderly women do before asking, "Can I help you?"

June's eyes move down toward her own feet. "I was," June glances up at Janet then back down at her feet. "I have, an appointment."

Janet's expression remains decidedly indifferent. "Checking into treatment?"

Looking at the older woman, June awkwardly wrings her fingers. "Yes."

Janet again assesses her from head to toe. "Drug Court?"

"Yes."

"Come on into the dining room and have a seat." Janet turns and waddles towards the row of dining room tables as she continues to talk to June with her back turned. "You have to meet with a counselor first, so we can make sure you're serious."

June sits at the first table she sees and waits - shaking tirelessly.

Another woman walks into the dining area with a warm and friendly smile on her face. "Hi, I'm Beth-the program coordinator."

She extends her hand, June stands, looks awkwardly at Beth's hand, then back down at her feet. "June."

Beth drops her hand and picks up June's duffle bag –provoking June's cardinal, defensive urges. She meets her glare with a gentle smile and reaches towards her arm. June recoils from her, bewildered by Beth's invasion. Beth gently smiles at her as she clutches her arm just below the elbow and tugs at her to walk. "It's ok, let's go to my office and talk." As they walk, June's eyes well up with tears. Beth gently prods, "What are these tears about?"

June shrugs shoulders and covers her face with one hand. "Not sure."

"Nervous?"

"Yes."

"I've heard a lot of residents describe it has having a bird in your stomach instead of butterflies, for me it was like a flock of birds, or anything in a large number trying to escape the confines of my insides."

June laughs. "You were a resident here once too?"

Beth smiles at her. "You'll find most of the staff here are recovering drug addicts because this is what we call a social model program, everybody teaches and everybody learns."

They walk through the building together and it is set up like a home with a living room, day room, music room, classroom and then a row of offices; they enter Beth's office. It is a cozy office with a nice comfortable couch, desk and a few chairs. Beth sits down at her desk while June sits directly across from her. The desk is covered in beautiful plants and family photos. "Why are you here?"

June shifts her position in the chair, and wrings her fingers "I'm on AOP and they said I had to go to a treatment center."

Beth prods at her, "Is that the only reason you're here?"

June stares at the floor and scratches her left wrist – piquing Beth's curiosity. "Why are you wearing a long sleeve shirt on such a hot day?"

"It's not that hot."

Beth smiles at her sarcastically. "Wanna try that again?"

"I like to keep my arms covered up."

"Why?"

June looks down at the floor again. "I use needles-there are bruises. It's embarrassing."

Beth moves over to the chair next to June's.

June recoils from her.

"Can I see?"

June crosses her arms.

"No."

"If you want to check into this treatment center, you're going to have to be more cooperative – won't you go to jail if we turn you away?"

Beth reaches out, gently grabs one of June's hands and pulls it over to her.

June relaxes and pulls up her sleeve to reveal her arm. It is covered in bruises and littered with track marks. There's a large lump on the back of her arm, a very large injection hole, and scabbed lacerations on her wrist.

Beth runs her fingers along June's arm. "What's this swelling here?"

"I missed a vein."

"Has a doctor looked at this yet?"

"No."

Beth makes her way down to the wrist lacerations. "Tell me what happened here."

Beth's voice slowly gives way to June's senses as she stares at her own wrist and way down she goes into the rabbit-hole of her mind. Where she has spent most of her conscious hours. It's always easier to hang out there than be in the present day of her life. This is the rabbit-hole to home. Her home with Tabitha – the hell she had been trying to die in for months. The hell that was so unbearable that dying was the greener grass on the other side. The hell of being a rock bottom JUNKIE with no hope of escape.

Tabitha was considerably older than June and had been a junkie for many, many years. She suffered from manic depression and frequented the local mental health hospital for monthly electric shock treatments. It was either the shock therapy, or the medications, or the drugs, but somehow Tabitha always had this white foam around the corners of her mouth, which was a fit pairing to her hair, frizzy, to the point of resembling a black cobweb. Crazy as she was, she was the only person in the world who knew the darkness of June's life and accepted her as she was. They were known around town as the "junkie bitches from hell" and they owned that shit...as much as a couple of rock bottom junkies can.

June sits on her bed searching for a vein as Tabitha crashes in through the bedroom door. "The cops are at the door!"

June looks at Tabitha in disbelief. "What?...Why?"

Tabitha laughs. "How the fuck should I know?"

June looks frantically around the room. "Shit, what do I do?"

Tabitha gestures towards the bathroom. "Just go in the bathroom and lock the door. I'll find out what they want."

4

June scratches at her arm while frantically looking around the room, "Just ignore them!"

"Fuck that, this is my house."

June opens her dresser drawer, full of bloody spoons and needles.

Tabitha leans in. "Uggh, welcome to my fuckin' nightmare."

June slams the drawer shut, runs into the bathroom, quietly shuts the door, locks it, and paces the bathroom in a panic. "What am I going to do?" she mutters to herself as she ponders a way to escape that house.

She can no longer remember a time in her life when she felt the need to smile. Those days had been gone for years – replaced by apathy, despair, shame and countless days wrapped in the fantasy of suicide. She wrings her fingers as she fixates on that dresser drawer in her room, littered with a plethora of bloody spoons and needles. She absolutely has to escape this house, somehow, someway. The bathroom window won't work because there are probably cops outside as well.

Desperately pacing, she focuses in on a razor, propped neatly on the side of the bathtub and is finally able to settle on the perfect escape plan. She turns on the bathtub water full blast and begins to pick at the plastic-trying to expose as much of the blade as possible muttering to herself, "The perfect escape plan."

She sinks into the warm water and begins cutting her wrist. Mesmerized by the sight of the blood she remains in a motionless gaze, until a loud crash from outside of the bathroom causes her to stir. She grabs the razor and cuts deeper – muttering to herself "faster…" as her stress intensifies to the cops shouting at Tabitha to get down on the floor.

BAM! BAM! BAM! "You can come out now-they're gone."

She looks at herself-submerged in a bathtub of bloody water and just stares for a minute. "What?"

"I said it's safe to come out now."

"How? I heard them tossing the place."

"I don't know what you think you heard but they're gone."

This is the moment, the moment of clarity, the "burning bush" as June stares at herself, submerged in blood and mutters, "What the hell have I done to myself?"

She climbs out of the bathtub and walks over to the bathroom mirror, covered in fresh steam. June uses her lacerated wrist to wipe the steam off of the mirror-leaving a bloody streak behind and stares deeply into her own eyes. She touches a scar above her right eyebrow, the bathroom gives way as she slides down the rabbit-hole into her childhood home.

The Kindergarten Years

The kindergarten years are easy.
They hold the beauty of never knowing what's to come or how long it will take to arrive.

As a child, I was very free spirited, and my father was the light of my life. I was musically inclined, a creative writer, and an avid reader – this was what I sank myself into. I didn't do so well in Math, History, or any of the boring school stuff and I wasn't so great at keeping up with my chores either. I was more about the wondrous world of magic, finding beauty in small spaces, and making friends with strange things like butterflies, little white flying bugs and praying mantis.

My father was the light of my life and saw to it that I always had everything that I needed. My mother, well, she was a fictitious character in my dreams. She was a GoGo dancer when her and my father met. I don't know how long they were together before they went their separate ways but one day she just dropped me off with him and disappeared.

My father was a bartender who lived in his car, unless he met a woman. He met lots of women. Usually what that meant is we would be living with whoever the new object of his affection was. When those relationships tanked, he'd send me to live with my aunt and uncle.

I loved being at my aunt and uncle's house because my cousins were basically my siblings. We fought, a lot. My fondest memory of those days were the times I picked a fight with one of my older cousins, then managed to give my aunt a special puppy dog look that got the other guy in trouble. Evil, I know.

I always looked forward to seeing my dad again, he was my super star, the one I pined after the most. One day when he came to pick me up, he advised that he was engaged to who would be my new stepmother. I eagerly hopped in the car to meet her.

She had kids of her own, so I was doubly excited to have two sisters and a brother. Even though they were a lot older than me it was very exciting. A trip to Disneyland exciting.

She was so nice and so beautiful, probably one of the most beautiful women I had ever seen. My new sisters were also very pretty and one of them was in beauty school so right away she wanted to do my hair.

Everything was great but they fought a lot, like many families do. In time, my stepmother and I started getting along less and less which was a circumstance that grew over the years leaving us in what I could only call a very up and down relationship.

As far back as I can remember I was always quite a daydreamer. Anytime I was unhappy I could slip into this daydream world and go anywhere that I wanted. Sometimes when I came back, I would write stories of where I had been. The daydreams were always very real, like alligators in the flooded streets of Pennsylvania, they were the stuff of movies.

I was also a sleepwalker, with frequent visitors of the deceased variety. Occasionally my visitors were recently deceased relatives. I quickly learned people got upset if I ran around saying I had just taken a long walk through the park with aunty, who died the other day, so I made it a point to keep that stuff to myself. A lot of people thought it was just my overactive imagination and scolded me for making up stories about the dead. I just ignored these people, what happened here was very natural to me.

I wasn't the best-behaved kid in the world and a lot of things happened in my childhood that probably contributed that but the biggest upheaval that spiraled me out of control was my GoGo Dancing mother. She magically appeared in my life one day and convinced me the grass would be greener on her side of the world in Oklahoma. She was lying to me, and her lies led me down a path that landed me in a lot of trouble.

Sadly, she betrayed me in an epic way that sent me into a tailspin. I found myself in juvenile hall and then in court custody, where I was remanded into a group home until the age of 18.

Three

Walking On A Dream

~⟨ ⟩~

*R*eality crashes in.
The illusion of the world that we think we live in is shattered as it collides
and kills the innocence.
Showing not once, but twice, but as many times as it takes.
No matter how bad we think it is.
It always gets worse.

Younger than most the men and women in the room, I felt out of place and bored to tears, as I fiddled around with a piece of birthday cake and listened to the traditional opening of an AA meeting: "This is the great obsession of every abnormal drinker. The persistence of this illusion is astonishing, many pursue it into the gates of insanity or death…"

Sandy plopped down in the chair next to me. "Try to pay attention, sweetie." Sandy was one of the counselors at the Talutha County group home I was stuck in until my 18th birthday. It felt like a prison sentence, I guess community living does that to a person. The system forced AA meetings, every Monday night. The counselors told me it was for my own good.

My only reprieve from the prison was public school, something to do with not being under any type of court mandated psychiatric care or medications. It would be wonderful to say that school was an area of my life that I excelled in, but truthfully, it was just easy access to Amber, which meant easy access to booze, pot, or whatever she could steal from her parents.

That, I felt, was pretty much the only thing that made my life worthwhile. Every day we hit the campus nature trail and the numbing party commenced.

I sat anxiously in class listening to the teacher speak inaudible gibberish as I stared at the clock on the wall, tapping my pencil to the sound of clock hands. They ticked down to noon and BAM! The buzzer rang – it was the official commencement of my cherished hour of freedom.

I rushed out of the classroom and hustled across campus to the river trail entrance to find Amber. "Got the goods?"

Amber smiled, pointed at her waistline, and we walked down the trail on the outskirts of campus.

Amber handed me a bottle of Vodka. "Bottoms up."

I took a swig. "I need to get the hell out of here."

Amber laughed. "The struggle is real with you, eh?"

I flipped her off as we walked down the trail to our favorite spot and sat down to share the bottle. Amber and I shared many of the same miseries, so it was no surprise that we found each other, buried in a similar hole of apathy, loneliness and the desire to run away forever.

Oftentimes we would sit out here and just daydream new lives for ourselves. We didn't get a whole lot of time to hang out together outside of school. Amber had the strictest of parents and me, well, I was a ward of the court...

"I hate my life," I said as I flopped down on my back to gaze at the blue sky.

Amber plucked randomly at the blades of grass. "I hate my step-dad," Amber said, then sprang up brimming with excitement. "Imagine this, we could run away and start new lives together all on our own." I have to admit that I was really curious.

"We don't need anyone or anything. Let's just live off the land."

"How?"

"I grew up on an Indian reservation. I know a lot about survival; we could go out into the forest and live on our own."

"Ok, where would we go?"

"That's the cool part; we can go anywhere we want."

"How would we get there?"

"We can just hitchhike to New York and have fun along the way."

I didn't want to admit that I had absolutely no idea what hitchhiking was, so I played along like I knew exactly what Amber was talking about. "Oh yeah, that's easy, I've done that a bunch of times."

Amber laid back down in the grass and told me stories of all of her adventures in hitchhiking until the bell rang, summoning us back to class. I turned to her and said, "Why don't we just leave, right now?"

"Hell yeah, that'd be sweet!"

I was ready, I started walking to the street. "Wait! We'd totally get caught if we left right now. Let's go tomorrow morning, we'll leave for school just like any other day but meet up at the corner of California and Market Street. Take the books out of your backpack and hide them under your bed. Fill up your backpack with clothes, food, anything that you can sneak out of the kitchen. That should last us a couple of days."

"But I don't ever want to come back."

"We need to travel light, dummy."

"Ok."

The rest of the school day dragged on even with a liquid lunch. I always found it humorous that I attended all of my afternoon classes drunk and my teachers never noticed. I wasn't sure if I was just invisible or they just didn't give a crap – whatever it was – trust and believe that I took full advantage of it.

The next morning, I replaced my books with clothing, hid my books under the bed, stole some snacks from the kitchen and left for school. We met up at a freeway on-ramp that was just beyond our bus stop. It worked because if anyone saw us walking they would naturally assume we were heading to school. I was nervous about getting spotted while we waited for a ride, but a man pulled over and offered us a ride within seconds.

The whole hitchhiking experience was an adventure in and of itself, men of all ages were quick to pick us up and drive us various distances. Amber had sex with most of them and their ages never seemed to matter. It was as if this was her intention all along or maybe there was just some kind of an unspoken party and sex rule involved in long-distance hitchhiking?

I didn't know what the truth was here, besides the fact that Amber seemed to be willing to share her body with just about anyone. I was really worried that sooner or later she was going to just leave me behind and take off with one of these guys. I eventually joined the party here and there for the sake of fitting in because I started to feel like a prude. I was worried that she was going to think I was dull and then she would definitely leave me behind. Luckily, there was Jack Daniels and after having enough of that joining the party was a lot easier.

As the days passed it seemed we weren't making a whole lot of progress. Here's how it went down: we'd hitchhike, men of various ages picked us up. Some of these men were old enough to be our fathers, yet somehow it always led to a party somewhere – waterfalls, houses, hotel rooms, you name it. Then the whiskey, sometimes drugs, then the clothes came off, then when it was over, we'd sleep, and the next day we'd be out there hitchhiking again.

Repeat.

Repeat.

Repeat.

I was getting so sick and tired of the routine. I was back to being a prude and I didn't care. This was not the deal when we left, this was not something I had ever agreed to. I would tag along, but I would sit and drink quietly in a corner. I was trying to find a way to tell her this needed to stop but I just didn't know how. I had racked up some cash along the way because a lot of these guys would express concern for our safety, imagine that? Then give us a little cash so that we could buy ourselves food during our travels.

My burning question at this point was simple: "where in the hell are we going?!?" My question slipped out as more of a demand, as I was following Amber down a busy city street in some unknown town. She was heading to the first freeway on-ramp she could find, while I was tagging along, as usual. Pounding headache, stomach twisted up in knots from starvation and drinking too much. "I said where the hell are we going!"

Amber gazed up at the sky as she casually strolled along. "Anywhere the wind blows us, I guess."

"No! We need a plan! I am starving, my head hurts, my feet are killing me." I pulled a wad of cash out of my pocket. "I still have all this money, we need to go sit down and eat. Then come up with a plan and do it."

"Let's just get to the freeway and find another ride." Amber looked at me with her typical attitude of not giving a shit. "Just be cool."

"NO!" I shouted and sat down in the middle of the sidewalk. I was infuriated. I crossed my legs and put my face in my hands as I rested my elbows on my knees. "We need to figure out where we are going and go there."

Amber came and sat down next to me but kept staring at the sky and just, wherever.

"What happened to the plan?" I pleaded to her with the utmost sincerity I could put out there. "We can't keep doing this, aren't you tired?"

Amber remained aloof and indifferent, for her it was only about the party. "That's why I'm trying to find our next ride, silly." She smiled at me. I was over that smile, I was tired of trying to play along to fit in, but she was my best friend. What would I do without her? I wish I could have seen the truth. I was so uncertain of what was happening here, I wanted desperately for her to keep being my friend, I wanted us to stick to the plan we had talked about before.

Why couldn't I see that the reason she couldn't seem to think reasonably, the reason she was constantly in a strange daze, was because this girl was in trouble. She was the last person on earth that I should have been listening to, but she was also my only friend. I was scared out there in the world with no adult guidance. I mean, I talked big about how I didn't need anyone, but the truth was I was terrified. I had always lived a very sheltered life. I was terrified Amber was going to figure out that I was the furthest thing from "cool," I was more of a spoiled child who grew up having every little thing I could ever want. I never had to fend for myself, and I had never been this far away from home. I had no idea what the world was like, but I was about to find out.

"Look, there's a little restaurant a couple of blocks down." I pointed at a Taco sign. "Let's just go there. We can get off of our feet for a little while and get something to eat. Then maybe we can talk about our next s„teps," I stuttered a little as my stomach jumped into my throat at the sight of the car, a white and gold two door Plymouth. It pulled over to the curb as the passenger side window rolled down. "Remember, Amber, we're going to eat."

Amber smiled at me with a look. It was the look of a disobedient child who wasn't going to do what she was supposed to do. She got up and walked towards the car.

"If you get in that car, you're going alone." I got up and started walking down the sidewalk.

I was trying to put my foot down. I didn't want to get separated but I had an unshakable feeling about the car, it creeped me out more than anything had ever creeped me out in my entire life. "June, they'll give us a ride to the Taco shop and buy us food."

I turned to see her leaning into the passenger side window talking to the guys, there were several of them, they looked older than high schoolers, but not too much older. Probably in their 20s? I didn't feel right about these guys, something just felt, off.

Amber was suddenly very energetic, excited. "Come on!" She waved me over as she climbed into the back seat of the car, squeezing into the middle. It was a two door, so the passenger had to get out and fold the seat forward so that she could climb in. All I could see was that she had absolutely no escape. I don't suppose she saw it that way because she was so down for whatever they would want to do to her that she probably felt there was nothing to be afraid of. I honestly feared for her life.

Suddenly I was guilt ridden. I knew that if we parted ways right there I would never see her again, was I ready for that? Would she even be ok? Maybe I was over reacting? He stood there, with the door open, waiting for me. "I just want to go to that restaurant," I said, pointing. It was only two blocks.

"We're buying, hop in."

I was calculating the situation as I walked over and figured I could easily jump out of the car if they didn't take us where they said they were supposed to, but when I got to the car he waved for me to get in first. "I want to sit by the door."

The man standing there with the door open smiled at me. "You have to sit in the middle."

"Why?" I stepped back.

"In case we get pulled over, just get in."

I hesitated.

The driver leaned over so that I could see him. "It's only two blocks, hop in."

Then of course Amber started making fun of me. "I thought you were hungry, get in the damn car!"

I didn't want to. I knew something was off, but I ignored my instincts and got in. The driver offered me a handshake. "I'm Adam."

I shook his hand. "June."

"Derrick," said the guy to the right of me.

The men in the back seat with Amber didn't offer any introduction as they were busy chatting with the flirty Amber. I kept a hawk's eye on the road ahead of me. I wish I could say I was surprised when they turned a corner and headed the opposite direction of the restaurant, but sadly I wasn't. "The restaurant was that way," I said, pointing over my shoulder.

Adam acted confused. "No, it's this way."

I was agitated but remained focused on the road ahead – wondering what was going to happen next and where he was taking us. "It was right back there."

"Oh, you don't want to go to any restaurant over there, I gotta way better place I'm taking you to."

Derrick laughed. "Yeah, we know the best spots around here."

"I didn't get in the car for this, pull over and let us out."

"Just relax, lady, we're gonna go eat."

Amber was quietly flirting with the men in the back seat and oblivious to what was going on. "Amber?"

My sentence was interrupted as Adam blasted the stereo. I wanted to turn off the stereo and talk but the truth is I was frozen in fear. I was afraid to move a muscle, I felt like any wrong or false move would trigger something. It's like running across a wild and dangerous animal. The first instinct is to run, but you know you can't get away in time and running just triggers their urge to chase and eat you. Sometimes the best survival choice is to stand completely still. I guess that is what was happening to me right then, as I stared at the passenger side door, knowing that with Derrick sitting there I'd never make it out of that car.

Adam drove till well past sunset for what seemed like an eternity. I finally reached for the stereo; he batted my hand away, so I shouted at him, "I want out of this car!"

"Fine!" He made a sharp left turn, drove up a steep, windy road, and stopped the car at a look-out point. He got out of the car and let me out.

I started walking, there was no civilization in sight. The roadways were too dark to see anything. I had absolutely no idea where I was. "Where in the hell are we?"

Adam laughed at me. "You said let you out of the car."

Amber finally spoke, and it seemed like the first I'd heard from her in a long time. "June, get back in the car, we're just having fun." It seemed like she was in on the joke. I was pissed. I didn't want to get back in the car, but I didn't know how to get to a phone or anything from out there in the middle of absolutely nowhere. I should have tried. I should have walked. I was honestly afraid of being out there in the dark with no flashlight. I would have gotten lost, but if I knew what was going to happen next, I like to think I would have taken my chances, but I still didn't want to leave Amber behind - I reluctantly got back into the car. "Please take us back into town."

Adam climbed back in. "How much would it cost us to kiss you?"

"I'm not kissing either one of you."

"Well, we don't want to kiss your mouth." Adam and Derrick reached

17

across me for a fist bump, then Adam pulled out a wad of hundreds. "How many of these?"

"None, you're not kissing me anywhere, let me out, I'll walk."

Adam put away his money, and started up the car. "You're not walking," he stated, then drove off down the winding dark roads. "I promised you dinner, that's where we're going, then maybe we can kiss you afterwards."

I felt a really heavy weight on my chest, pressure. I didn't know where this was going but definitely nowhere good. Adam proved my instincts were right as he began a strange little game began. He would drive for a while and then ask me, "You ready to get out of the car?" Then he'd pull off into some field, in the middle of nowhere and say, "How about here?" He did this repeatedly, toying with me, then the money would come back out. He was offering more and more. Then he offered $100 for a kiss on the lips, $500 for a kiss wherever they choose. I just ignored him, I was in panic mode and had never been through anything like this in my entire life.

After his unaccepted propositions, he would repeat the same steps, put the money away and start driving again. I knew this was a sick game. I knew I was outnumbered and overpowered. I just wondered how this was going to end and I wondered what would happen if I just said yes. "Ok, we're finally here, for real this time." I fearfully waited to find out where he was taking us as he made a sharp right-hand turn and drove down a long dirt road. I assumed there would be a house at the end of the road but it was just a corn field.

He drove deep inside and parked. The only thing for miles were dirt roads and corn, lots and lots of corn. "Dinner time," he laughed as he parked the car. He and the other guys got out. All of them. I stayed in the car to try and keep as much distance from myself and them as possible. I turned around to talk to Amber in the back seat.

"Come on, I wanna get away from these weirdos!"

She was in a strange state, she looked like she was asleep, but her eyes slightly opened. "What??" Her speech was slurred and her eyes glazed over. I had been partying with her for a while now and I had never seen her look this way. I didn't know what to think at the time, but I tried to talk her into getting out of the car.

"These guys are really weird, get out of the car and we'll find someone else to party with."

"I just," she started falling down towards the floorboard of the car. "I happy here." Just then the guys that had been riding in the back seat came back to rejoin her in the car. I got out as everyone was piling in and Adam put his arm around me.

"Well?"

"I just need to go pee."

I forced myself to smile at him. "Then we can kiss."

"You sure about that?"

"I'm really hungry, I thought you were taking me to dinner?" I tried to be friendly in my first attempt at acting, as I casually worked my way towards the corn field. " My stomach really hurts."

"When you come back, we'll get something to eat, after," he said, as he flashed some money at me.

I smiled at him. "Ok," I said, and kind of glanced over at Amber before catching myself and smiling back at Adam again. "I'll just be a minute."

"Yeah, I know." He laughed with a condescending look on his face. He knew I was too scared to wander far, in the middle of a corn field but he forgot to consider one thing. Anyone who truly knows that they are in a desperate fight for their lives will generally stop at nothing to escape. I couldn't worry about Amber anymore, as hard as it was. I had to leave her behind if I was going to save myself and to be honest, I knew from the moment I saw that car pull up that something was off. I knew that if I left Amber alone I would never see her again, so I knew that this guy was never going to leave me alive.

I walked into the corn field and squatted – watching their every move. Adam and Derrick turned to talk to each other as I started trying to scan my whereabouts under the light of the full moon. I saw headlights on a busy road, it was quite a ways away and the only real cover to hide in was the corn field. I took off running, deep into the corn field.

The blades of corn scratched and cut my skin as I zig zagged through. I wasn't sure where they were, I wasn't looking back. I just knew if I kept zig zagging through the corn there was no way they would find me but I had to get to the busy road. I heard the car, the engine revved and I stopped as I spotted the car, flying down the little dirt road that ran alongside the corn field. I instinctually knew when to drop to the ground and wait, as they slowed to a stop and shined a flashlight exactly where I had been standing.

I waited, the car took off again. I ducked in and out with the flow of their search. It seemed there was not going to be any escape but I spotted a few sparse trees that almost spanned the length of the field that stood in between the corn field and the roadway. My instincts were my friend, as I managed to time each move, barely escaping their sight.

Then my luck ran out, I was at the road, but there were no cars in sight and no trees to provide shelter. The Plymouth cut through the field and was headed straight for me. I ducked the headlights and dove into the shadows as I low crawled into a storm drain. They parked parallel to the road and I heard the car doors open. "You shoulda taken care of that bitch instead of toying with her all night."

"Don't forget who's in charge here."

"I'm fucking serious, asshole."

"Ya wanna end up in the same hole as the other one?"

I could hear them walking around above me, the storm drain wasn't long, I was barely out of view, their flashlights kept shining on my legs and then they stopped. "Hold on."

I knew it was over, why in the hell did I get into that car? Why did I think I could help Amber if I got into that car? Why did I follow her that way? Why was she so ready to abandon me? I couldn't handle the reality of the moment.

"June?"

I was so startled I almost let out a scream, I clasped my hand over my mouth at the sight of Amber, sitting across from me, back at the school, in our spot on the nature trail.

I dropped my hand and relaxed for a minute as I realized I had done it again. Slipped away into my magical place of daydreams, except something about Amber was different. "What's wrong, June?"

I wiped a tear from my face. "Nothing." I laughed sarcastically. "I'm just sitting here waiting to join you."

"I'm sorry."

Suddenly I was back in the storm drain, woken from my state of disassociation by the sound of the car doors slamming shut. They left. I started to slide out of the storm drain and then a fear struck me that it was too good to be true. So, I resumed my spot, and stayed as quiet as possible. For a long time, there was not a single sound for miles around, until the silence was finally interrupted by Adam. "Let's just go get rid of this one. I doubt she'll make it outta here anyways."

My heart jumped into my throat as I heard the car doors open, and close. Realizing they had been waiting there the entire time, I was so relieved I waited. After that scare, I kept waiting and didn't even dream of making a sound or coming out until daylight.

An experience like that is unforgettable. It was a moment in time when I felt that my life was truly about to end. I didn't understand what my little check out moment was with Amber but I suspected she was dead, if not yet then she was soon to be. I felt really bad but I also felt relieved to have escaped. It was a strange combination of emotions that proved to slowly destroy me.

My instincts were the driving force of my survival that day but I seemed to lose the ability to listen to them after that. The events that occurred next were even more horrendous than I could have ever imagined and honestly, I felt like maybe it was my Karma for saving myself that led to the most hellish two weeks of my life.

Four

The Deepest Scars

The Deepest Scars
The deepest scars in life rest deep beneath the surface.
Washed away by nothing.
Bleeding out onto everything.
Setting forth a metamorphosis that will forever remain unchanged.
These are the adventures in hitchhiking.

I sat on a bench, in a daze as I looked, but didn't see, the rush hour traffic whipping by. It had been a long, long, road since I left Amber. I could not believe I went through all of that, and escaped, just to dive back into the exact same situation, over and over again. All I could think about was how guilty I felt leaving her behind and that the events that happened next were the universe's way of punishing me for doing it. I wasn't supposed to survive. It was clear to me now. I had no idea what to do, what to think, or who I even was anymore. I wasn't even sure how long I had been away from home.

"Excuse me?" I heard a male voice talking to me, but I was too far gone to care. "Excuse me?" I heard a police radio and finally composed myself enough to see who was talking to me. It was a police officer.

I tensed up. "I did what he told me to do, go away."

"Why aren't you in school?" He stood in front of me with a little notepad.

His question completely baffled me. How in the hell could he be asking me about school! I mean school of all things, that was a lifetime ago. That was when my life was real, that was when my life was, a life. I no longer had a life anymore, I was an object, a piece of trash, a nothingness. "How old are you?"

I could hear him, but his question didn't register with me. "What?"

"What is your name?"

He kind of startled me again, I actually had to think about the answer, I just started crying. "I left her behind."

"You're gonna need to answer some of my questions or I'll take you in to the station."

His threat enraged me, just another piece of shit trying to get me alone in his car. "I'm not going with you anywhere!"

He stepped over to his patrol car and talked to someone on his radio. Nothing was happening in real time to me as it all zipped by in a blur, but a little while later I was in a hospital room. There were female officers, counselors and doctors. The officer wanted me to tell him everything that happened and where it happened. It was important to him to try and help me but I was useless, as usual.

I told him about feeling like I had to leave Amber because she refused to come with me. "I'm really, really sorry but I left her." He wanted full descriptions of the men and told me he wanted me to come to the station when the hospital releases me, to look at mugshots and see if I could identify them. "Yes, I can try." I told him what the car looked like. "I tried to go to the police sooner but the guy who was giving me a ride didn't take me." I honestly felt guilty, like I had committed a crime because I left her.

"I flagged down the first car I saw at sunrise, it was a couple, they were in formal wear, I guess they had just come from a prom? They said they would take me to their house first for clothes."

"Why did you need clothes?"

"I don't know.

"When we got there, they offered to let me use their shower. I definitely needed one."

"Why did you need a shower?"

"I was dirty and bloody."

"Whose blood was it?"

"I think it was mine?"

He just kept writing down what I was saying, and the more I talked the more nervous I got – convinced I was in trouble so I sped up and abbreviated the rest. "When I was in the shower he came in there with me and we had sex. He said the police station was closed but he would take me in the morning and he dropped me off nearby. He gave me money so that I could get something to eat. I looked for the police station but I couldn't find it. Then another guy offered to take me, he said it was only a couple of minutes away but then he drove me somewhere else. He wanted to give me money for sex, I said no cause I'm not a hooker, but he said he wasn't letting me go until I did. I did what he wanted but I didn't take the money, I swear."

"You have done nothing wrong here, June, I just want to know what happened so I can go do my job. Please tell me everything you can remember about him."

"I can't, I mean, I can tell you more about the other guys."

"What other guys?"

"The truck driver. He drove one of those huge trucks, he had short brown hair, a beard, and wore a flannel shirt and jeans. He was your age and looked like a lumberjack. Like I've seen in commercials. He said he would give me a ride home but then he pulled over on the side of the road to go to the bathroom. Then he opened my door and told me to get into the sleeper or he would break my neck."

"What happened?"

"He made me, you know."

"Did he rape you?"

"He said if I bit it he would kill me, so I didn't bite."

"Ok, did you get his name?"

"No."

"What kind of truck was it?"

"A big one, it was red."

The officer was writing everything down. "I need as many details you can give me."

"That's really all that I know."

I could see the disappointment on his face. "Is there anything else?"

There was actually a lot more but I was honestly too ashamed to talk about it. The fact is that ever since I left Amber I was climbing into one car after another. At first, I was trying to get to the police so that I could tell them what happened to Amber. It's just that every single man who picked me up wanted to pay me for sex. I was not a prostitute, I said no but they always persisted. I already knew what it would lead to, but I still said no anyways. Then they would threaten me and I would comply for the sake of my own survival.

Sometimes when they dropped me off they would still hand me the money and I would just refuse. This happened several times until I decided I would not take any more rides from just anyone. I knew what I should really do is call home but I dreaded doing that because of the world of trouble I was going to be in. So, I decided that it was time to go home but I would get myself there. I just needed to find a safe person to give me a ride. It was impossible to accept that every single person who offered me a ride would be the same level of bad as the rest of them. Most of them were a lot older so I was thinking a younger person would be a safer choice. Someone closer to my age, but a little older because I was only 13.

I ended up accepting a ride from someone that I thought was really cute, he couldn't have been much older than me. It happened again though, he offered me money. I didn't want to know if he was as bad as the rest. I wanted to tell myself that I didn't make another mistake getting into that car. I wanted to feel like I had a choice for a change, like this wasn't another strike of my own stupidity, so I accepted the money as if that was exactly what I was doing out there on the street.

Afterwards I sat on a bus bench, in tears. Another person stopped by, there were two of them. They reminded me of some kids I went to school with back home. They couldn't have been more than a couple of years older than me. They asked me what was wrong and I sort of told them. They said they were on their way home with groceries, as they were having a big family dinner and party. They showed me the groceries and asked if I was hungry. The truth is, I was literally starving to death. It was hard to resist the food. They assured me they would not do to me what any of the other guys did and that their mother was at the house and she could get me home. The more they talked the nicer they seemed. I got in.

They treated me very gingerly as they were explaining every turn and the driver said, "Here we are, that's the house." I was relieved to see the bustling house, lots of people, they were BBQ'ing outside, I was starving. They pulled over, but never came to a complete stop before pulling away from the curb.

The guy in the passenger seat asked the driver, "Where are you going?"

The driver responded, "I gotta make one more stop."

It sounded to me like the situation was taking a turn for the worst. It also didn't sound like both of the men were in on it so I had hopes that is wasn't anything bad. We drove out to an empty field. The driver got out and made me get out with him. He was one of the worst of all of the men I had to deal with up to that point. He made very clear that we were too far away for me to run, too far out for anyone to help me, he had a gun in the trunk, and if I did not take of my clothes and bend over he would put a bullet in my head.

The passenger pleaded with him to leave me alone and they actually argued about how long it had been since he had gotten laid. The passenger didn't touch me, but he didn't intervene either. I looked at my options and he was right. There was nowhere to go except where he told me to, so I did. Then they dropped me off exactly where they picked me up.

I sat, frozen in time, shocked about the ordeals that I had been through out there alone and wondered what Amber's ordeal was like. I ignored countless scumbags who tried to lure me into their cars, then a police officer pulled up. He was not in a patrol car, he was in a regular car, but he showed me his badge and offered to help me get home.

I will never know if he was tricking me or if he was actually a cop, but he took me to his house and raped me. Causing damage to my wrists in the process he was more aggressive than any of the other men.

I walked down the street completely stunned about all that had happened, utterly humiliated, upset with myself that I was such a moron. I blamed myself for getting into all of those cars, I blamed myself for running away. This was all my fault and I had suffered some heavy consequences. I needed to pee. I didn't have any sense of self or privacy for my body anymore, so I didn't seek out a bathroom, I just mindlessly dropped my pants and peed in the middle of a busy street, with onlookers gasping. I shouted, "Fuck off!" then I walked over to the bus bench where the officer found me.

That suddenly reminded me, he was still sitting there waiting for me to answer him. I looked at him for a moment, then decided the rest of my story of what happened to me out there was something I would take with me to my grave.

"No, there was nothing else."

Five

A Watery Grave

The best moments in life are found in the simplest of things,
slipping away over time to be swallowed whole by something larger:
apathy, darkness, and despair.
It's the feeling of being trapped, in a watery grave, with one wing stuck to the pavement
and no amount of strength can break it free.
The only hope resting in the kindness of another.
Kindness...
A sentiment forgotten by this world a long, long, time ago.

I had finally turned 18 and was back in my hometown. My dad had let me move back home while I worked and saved money to live on my own. He wanted me to enlist in the Army. It's what he had done when he was my age and he fondly looked upon it as the smartest move he ever made. He told me about all of the benefits of it and he thought it was the smartest move for me at that point.

I felt like I had just served a really long prison sentence and I didn't want to turn right around and sign up for another institution so I said, "Ok, I'll sign up." He took me to the recruiting office and I filled out all of their paperwork. I was all set to go as soon as I took their basic entry tests. I failed the math test, repeatedly.

"If you don't want to do it why don't you just say so? Instead of going out of your way to waste everyone's damn time?" My aggravated father asked me.

"I suck at math, I'm not doing it on purpose," I insisted.

He just looked at me, reading me, trying to decide if he believed me. It would be surprising to me that he read me as being full of shit because I swore I was doing my best, but the truth was I seriously didn't want to go to the Army.

This little issue festered and he gave me an ultimatum. I had a set date to be signed up for Boot Camp or I had to move out of the house. I waited until the last day and then I moved out of the house. I was so wrapped up in my lies that I didn't even know I was sabotaging it on purpose. I had been a different person since the hitchhiking ordeal and very disassociated from my emotions. If I had known the path that I was headed down, I would have broken into Boot Camp and handcuffed myself to a tree. One of the most valuable lessons I learned from that is to listen to my elders, they actually do know what is best most of the time. Still, I wandered off into the unknown, making up my mind that I was going to begin my life as an adult and I was going to do everything my way.

I had developed enough street smarts that I never got into a car with a stranger, unless I had a weapon handy. Any old weapon would do. I had taken self-defense classes and learned a thing or two about how to deal with, um, the kind of thing I used to not know how to deal with. One of the most upsetting things I learned in my class was "the perps are gonna tell you they have a gun, but if you don't actually see a gun, then it is just a scare tactic. They will say anything they can, to scare you into cooperating." This angered me, as I realized that not only had I been violated, they were preying on my fears so that I would cooperate.

A lot of the guilt and shame I felt in relation to those incidents was about the fact that I didn't fight for myself. I felt like I was such a weak person. It would have felt better to fight for a chance than to just give them what they wanted. At the same time, the fact that I ran away and left my best friend behind created guilt and fear that plagued me too. I was a person who was very much at odds. In any case, the new me was never going to allow anything like that to happen again. I had my mind made up that anyone who tried would have to kill me first and the attitude I had was apparent to the world.

My days in the group home I experienced episodes of blackout rage. It didn't take a lot to set me off but once I was set off, everything went black, I did a lot of damage, and then when it was over I came back. This was a tendency I now possessed and part of it was the armor I carried around to protect myself from being hurt by anyone else, ever again.

I also liked to hook up with bad-boy boyfriends. I felt like I was safest with them, primarily guys who'd just did some time. The more the bad-boy the better. The reason for this? Contrary to rumors, a lot of these ex-convicts are known for beating down sex offenders, so I was naturally drawn to them after my many ordeals.

My latest one was not fresh out of jail, he hadn't even been in any trouble yet, but his uncle was on parole. His family was hiding from the law so they lived off the land. When I say that I mean literally, off the land, they lived on a boat. I really liked all of them a lot so I went and stayed on the boat with them.

It was pretty much a non-stop party and everything was awesome, they were like a second family to me. We played quarters and drank beer like it was going off the market soon. Nobody used any drugs, everyone just loved their beer. It was me, my boyfriend Justin, his uncle John, his mother Tina and his 13-year-old cousin Randy. I connected with Randy a lot, being that he was the age I was when my childhood ended.

John and Tina worked at a restaurant in a nearby resort. The boat we lived on was anchored on the river, out and away from the roads; "as long as we are anchored we don't have to pay any fees to live here" is what they explained to me. The only way to come and go from the boat was with a little boat called a dingy.

One morning I woke up all alone, I found a note that everyone went to the resort. I laid back down and passed out. Shortly afterwards, I woke to someone peeking around on the boat. I got up, grabbed a knife from the kitchen, and went looking for the trespasser. It was some yuppy looking guy. "Whoa!" he exclaimed when I startled him. "I don't want any trouble."

"Get gone."

The man walked briskly to the edge of the boat while talking to me over his shoulder. "Is this your boat?"

"Who's asking?" I followed him over to the edge and saw his boat, next to mine, and as he climbed over to it I saw a woman and a little kid waiting for him on it so I put the knife down.

"I'm sorry, I was just really curious and wondering if it was for sale?"

"I don't know but if you want to give me a ride to the resort I can introduce you to the owner."

"How far is the resort?"

"Just around the riverbend."

His wife looked at him like he was crazy, shaking her head and whispering under her breath. Undeterred, he said, "Sure, we'll take you."

I boarded their boat. It was awkwardly silent as he and his wife softly bickered back and forth on the drive over. He pulled up to the dock to let me off. "We're not interested in the boat, but have a good one."

I didn't care, I knew it wasn't for sale but I needed a ride to the party. I said, "Ah, bummer, see ya" and hopped onto the dock and searched for the others. I found them, partying at the end of one of the docks, and I joined them.

Uncle John walked over. "Hey, your mom asked me to tell you to keep it down out here, we don't want to lose our jobs over all the underage drinking going on."

I smiled at him. "I'll make sure they quiet down."

"Thanks, sweetie," John said as he hustled off, talking over his shoulder, "dishes wait for no one."

There was a homeless guy hanging out on one of the docks, well, more like leaning. He was the town drunk and could barely stand. Justin decided to give him a bad time, so he walked over and kicked him. "What are you doing out here, old man?"

The man was so inebriated that he barely moved a muscle. Randy laughed. "Dude's fucking wasted!"

Justin pulled out a gallon sized bottle of Vodka and waved it in front of him. "Don't you want some more of this?"

The man just looked at him, bewildered.

Ryan seemed to be very amused by his brother's bullying. "You should make him drink it," he urged.

I was really disgusted with both of them.

Justin seemed to be feeding off of Ryan's thirteen-year-old excitement. "What's this?" He quickly snatched a wallet that was peeking out of the man's pocket.

"Give it back!" he barely slurred out.

I couldn't stand to watch this anymore. "Give him back his wallet."

"No." Justin smiled. "Not until he drinks this entire bottle of Vodka."

The man mustered up all the strength he had to sit up and reach for his wallet. "I'm not drinking anything, just give it back." He failed and fell back down on the dock – emptyhanded.

"Drink it! Drink it!" Randy started chanting along with other teenagers nearby.

"Oh my God, leave him alone!" I got up and charged Justin. "Give me that guy's wallet!"

I reached for it but Justin pulled it away from me and snapped, "Sit down you fucking bitch!" then he shoved me down. I was shocked, he had never spoken to me or treated me that way. "I thought you were cool June, just fucking kick rocks, I don't want you around anymore."

"What? Since when?"

"Since now. That's why I took off without your ass this morning, you're weighing me down."

"Fine, I'll go but leave that guy alone – he looks half dead already."

"You want me to leave him alone?"

"Yes!"

"Fine, you drink it and I'll leave him alone."

"Are you serious?"

"Yes, I dare you to drink it. Do it, and I'll leave him alone. But someone has to drink it, it's either you or it's him."

I had the power to save someone else from being hurt by random strangers. With the guilt of Amber weighing on me all these years I wasn't about to make the same mistake twice. Walking away was just like running away while Amber was still in that car. It didn't matter that I didn't know this homeless drunk.

What mattered is that people have a right to be treated a certain way, nobody should be violated in any way, shape or form. I clearly suffered from a desperate need to save someone. I didn't know it until that moment, but it was constantly tugging at me, all the time. I didn't think the Vodka would hurt me. "Hand it over," I growled as I snatched it from Justin, "but give him back his wallet first."

Justin returned the wallet. "You have to chug the whole bottle, all of it."

A small crowd gathered around and cheered me on as I finished off the half gallon of Vodka. By the time I swallowed the last drop I was totally smashed. I sat down on the dock, laid back and watched the sky spin while listening to the echoed voices of everyone around me and the man I just saved said, "Look what you guys did to that poor girl, is she ok?" They ignored him and kept laughing.

Then I heard John say, "I told you that you guys had to be quiet! You're gonna get us fired!" Through blurry vision I saw him lean over the top of me, blocking out the blue sky. "Are you?….ah shit, you're drunk. Shit! I gotta get you outta here, sweetie."

I laid there, smiling at him, the world spinning, as he hoisted me up and slung me over his shoulder. The ground looked funny as he carried me down, and off of the property. I had to close my eyes as everything started spinning. He laid me down in a field across from the resort then leaned back over me. "I'll be back to check on you sweetie, you're safe."

"Bye!" I yelled. I tried to wave but my arms just felt too heavy.

His face disappeared and all I could see was the swirling sky again. Suddenly all the lights went out. After a little while I realized I had closed my eyes, and when I finally managed to open them again Randy was standing over me, pulling off my clothes. I couldn't speak or move my arms or legs. I couldn't do anything. It was as if my entire body had fallen to sleep, except my brain and my eyes.

I struggled and finally shouted, "No!" but he ignored me.

I could not believe this little twerp was on top of me. This brat that I could totally take. I focused really hard on my right hand as if using my mind to move it and I managed to slap him once, it was feeble, and my limp arm fell back down. So, he punched me in the face, hard, and then proceeded to rape me. He said some horrible things to me and I was surprised to hear that he despised me so much.

I wanted to fight harder and just couldn't. It was the most powerless feeling in the world, like being paralyzed from head to toe while some sick son of a bitch violates your body – fortunately his violation was over in just a minute since he was most likely a virgin. "If you tell anyone about this I'll fucking kill you!" He said as he zipped up his pants and left.

I cried as I stared up at the sky, hoping that there wouldn't be any more visitors. John never came back to check on me but as the sun was setting I began to feel my limbs a little more. I slowly pulled myself upright into a sitting position, sinking my fingers into the mud I could feel it packing in under my long fingernails as I rose up and managed to get onto my feet.

I stumbled, veered and fell down a couple of times as I headed back over to the resort. I had to climb a flight of stairs to get out of the field I was in. I fell, I looked down at my stinging knee and saw the blood oozing out of it.

I stepped out into the road, startled as car tires squealed, almost hitting me. I focused intently on getting to my destination as it rapidly whipped around me. I walked onto the patio of the restaurant and spotted Tina. I screamed, "Randy raped me!"

Tina rushed over, yanked a table cloth off of a table and held it in front of me. "Calm down!"

I was hysterical, I just kept screaming the same thing over and over again. It was pent up rage from everything that happened in the past, coupled by the present, amped up by the Vodka. "Randy raped me! Randy raped me!

Randy raped me!"

"SHUT UP!" Tina slapped me so hard that I fell down, hard.

I stayed down on the ground and cried.

Six

Insanity Run Deep

nsanity Runs Deep
The confines of the mind get smaller and smaller until there is no escape.
Sinking deeper and deeper into the gates of insanity, until there is nothing left but
the suicidal years of a hopeless Junkie.

When I woke up I was having trouble seeing clearly, everything was blurry. I fixated my eyes on some little droplets of liquid I saw, as I struggled to hold them open. It was hard to determine where I was or what I was seeing, as my eyes battled a stinging sensation of bright lights after passing through a really dark tunnel. A shooting ping of fear struck my groin as I immediately assumed I'd gotten myself into some trouble, but the ease of lifting my free arms told another story. A nurse walked into the room.

"Oh, you're finally awake, how are you feeling?"

"Shitty, where am I?"

"What's the last thing you remember?"

I had absolutely no recollection of anything that has happened since I woke up on the boat. Straining, I mentally tried to re-trace my steps. In rapid flashes I remembered the bum, I remembered the vodka, then, I remembered "him" on top of me. Him, the 13-year-old brat with no right to live, the piece of shit kid that I could totally take in a fight that managed to get to me, then that bitch Tina screaming at me, and slapping me. The memory gave me such a startle that I opened my eyes and rubbed my face as if it literally just happened - all over again.

I stared at my nurse. "How did I end up in here?"

"You were found unconscious on the side of the road, alcohol poisoning."

I laid my head back, to close my eyes and remember the psychopath who I always thought was so nice, hoisting me over his shoulder, and shoving me into his car like I was nothing but a rotten sack of potatoes. These are the people that I thought were so great, my home away from home, my adventure living on a pirate ship where everyone did their part. I looked to the nurse for retribution. "I was raped."

"We know, we did a rape kit." The nurse changed out my IV bag. "I'll go get you the doctor, and there's a detective waiting to speak with you, too."

"Thank you."

After the nurse left I relaxed into the bed, feeling lost, confused, and absolutely idiotic for letting it happen to me, again. Who in the world would be so stupid that they put themselves back in the same situation, over and over again? Me. That's who. There isn't a single person on this earth who can be trusted, I don't care who they are, where they come from, or what they do.

Every single human being is capable of the worst, and I for some reason am drawn to these people like a magnet. I knew what I had to do, I had to end it, I had to end me, I had absolutely no reason for living. My... "Hi, Ms., um what is your name?" MY private rant was rudely interrupted by el jerko in the white coat.

I choked a little as I tried to answer him "June."

He reached to shake my hand but I didn't feel like it. I stared at his hand and waited for him to give up. "Ok, so we ran the rape kit on you and have been waiting for you to wake up so that we can discuss preventative measures."

I stared at him again, completely confused about what he was going on about.

"Some victims of rape like to be proactive in terms of pregnancy. I can offer you something called The Morning After. What it does is terminate any risk of pregnancy. It's not 100% effective but most of the time it is very effective. Is that something you're interested in?"

"Yes."

"You have really high levels of alcohol in your system, do you remember how much you drank?"

"Vodka, a large ½ gallon bottle."

"Well, luckily there doesn't appear to be any damage, we have had you on a saline IV for hydration. After we give you The Morning After pill you are free to go. Do you have anyone you'd like me to call?"

"No."

"Here's the card for the detective, give him a call if you'd like to make a statement."

I accepted the card, took the pill, and anxiously rushed out of the hospital with absolutely nowhere to go. I wandered the streets for a little while until heading over to my friend Heather's house. I hadn't seen her in a long time but I used to babysit for her and thought I could count on a sympathetic shoulder from her until I figured out my next move.

I stopped into a grocery store to use the bathroom, and when I passed through the alcohol aisle, the sudden aroma of Vodka filled the air and I vomited. This became the case for me, every single time I saw a bottle of alcohol, any brand, the sudden need to hurl overpowered me. Something about that alcohol poisoning had completely ruined the party.

My life was a train wreck of misery, despair, and tragedy. The only escape I had was the booze. What in the world was I supposed to do? All I wanted was to escape, but it was as if I was suddenly allergic. It had been two weeks since my "incident" and I had not had a single drop of any mood or mind-altering substances.

I had never used anything other than smoking pot and drinking. My party, my escape, my everything was stripped away in one fell swoop. What about that awesome boyfriend that led me to the ship in the first place? I could hardly remember what happened but I vaguely remembered him randomly deciding to break up with me because I cared about the random homeless person.

This was one of the many things I hated about myself. I cared way too much about people I don't even know. This was always the case, ever since I was really young. I could not understand where it came from, and it seemed that nobody cared about me in return. My life was a whirlwind of confusion and I HAD TO HAVE MY ESCAPE.

One day as I found myself back out on the streets, again, I decided to loiter on the front lawn of a laundromat. James walked up and sat down on the grass in front of me. I only knew him from a couple of parties I had been to but had never really sat and held a conversation with him.

"How's it going?" James tried to kick off some small talk.

"Well, it's pretty shitty, but same as always."

James pulled a small plastic baggie out of his pocket, full of a white powdery substance. "Want some?"

"Depends on what it is."

"You never did any speed before?"

"Nah, man, I heard it fucks up your nose."

"Come on into the laundry room."

I followed him into the laundry room and he drew some lines on one of the machines. "One line of this and ALL of your problems will go away."

"Seriously?" I have to admit that I was both surprised and skeptical.

"Yes," he replied as he rolled up a dollar bill and snorted a line off of the machine, then handed it to me, "just hold one side of your nose and inhale."

I took the makeshift straw and snorted the line. It burned like hellfire in my nose, my forehead, and my eyes. I actually cried a little from the force of the drugs going through my sinuses. Then it hit my throat and made me gag a little. It reminded me of jumping into a pool and letting the water rush up my nose, except it also had a peculiar taste. "I doubt this will make all my problems go away." I handed him back his dollar bill.

He laughed at me. "Just wait," he promised, then he left after saying, "See ya, I gotta be somewhere."

My friend Heather showed up and saw the remnants of the meth on the machine. "Did you seriously just do drugs?"

I smiled at her and shrugged.

"Who the hell gave this to you?"

"A friend."

"Well," Heather said as she blew the rest of it off of the machine, "I quit that shit a long time ago, nothing but trouble; also, if we're going to Graffiti Nights, we gotta go. It's a four-hour drive."

I followed Heather to her car. "So you're not mad at me anymore?"

"You can't stay at the house anymore, but you can sleep in my car at night till you find a new place."

"Groovy."

Heather looked at me confused, and I just laughed at her. I guess the first line of meth was starting to kick in because I was suddenly in a really good mood. The drive to Graffiti Nights was shockingly short, as I talked and talked and talked. Heather giggled at me a lot. "Are we already here?" I said. "I thought this was a long drive."

Heather laughed. "It's been four hours, you have been talking non-stop the whole way."

"Wow, I guess he was right about this stuff."

"Who was right about what?"

"He said meth would take all my problems away."

Heather laughed at me again but I don't think she knew I was actually very serious. It was literally the perfect drug. The moment I snorted a line all of my problems went away because of one simple factor: I stopped feeling. I was able to disconnect from my miserable existence and go along for the Meth Ride as long as the high lasted, and the best part? I was very self-aware of my surroundings. I had finally found my true-life partner.

Seven

Sinking Deeper

*S*inking Deeper
The depths of the ocean run true blue with beautiful enemies and long-lost friends.

We think we have found foundation for a day, only for it to fall off and drift miles away.

We think we have found salvation for a day, but it falls off and drifts miles and miles away.

Sinking.

Sinking.

The pressure is too much.

We will all implode into dust.

If it sounds like I had a love affair with Methamphetamine, that's because I did. I fell in love with the drug, at first line. I had fun all night long, until the rush of that first line wore off. While sleeping in Heather's car I made up my mind that I had to get more. She had left the keys behind so I helped myself and off I went. I had never had a driving lesson and did not know the first thing about cars or the city.

I drove around for a while, scanning the sidewalks for someone that I could get a line from. Sooner or later the car stopped running, and I had to roll to the side of the road. I suspected it may be out of gas but I had no idea how to check, no idea where the gas tank was, and no money to speak of anyways.

I found a payphone and called Heather collect. "I think the car is out of gas."

"Where is my car!"

"I don't know."

"I can't believe you did this to me! I was trying to help you! You know how important it is! WHERE IS MY CAR!"

The moral of the story here is that Heather and I met working at a dead-end McDonalds job. The only reason she worked there was to pay for this car. She lived with her family so that she could afford the car - her biggest accomplishment in life. I was in a meth-induced haze and had absolutely no clue where I, or her car was. I could still hear her yelling through the earpiece as I quietly hung up the payphone and called my aunt collect. "I really need a couch for a couple of days. I did drugs and I've been up all night. Can you come and get me?" I gave her a few landmarks and she picked me up.

My first night at her place was the first time I saw a movie that I have since then never been able to un-see. It's called "Clean and Sober" with Michael Keaton. I remember it being a really good movie, but I think the only reason the movie intrigued me was because it featured a drug similar to my new love, Methamphetamine. I watched the whole movie in hopes to see some and muttered to myself, "Boy, that guy's got it rough."

I spent most days plotting and planning my new relationship with methamphetamine. My aunt was kind enough to let me stay long-term in her spare bedroom as long as I gave her a ride to the bar and back – it worked for us.

Eventually I got a housekeeping job at a nearby hotel, they were still hiring, so I took that opportunity to try and make peace with Heather. I told them about her, called her down there and she got a job there too. All was forgiven, she loved me again. Then things got even better. Our first day cleaning together Heather pulled me into one of her rooms and pulled out a baggie of meth. "Wanna do a line together?"

I smiled at her, happy to be on the same page again.

"You know I do."

The workplace became the party place and each day a new beginning – of drugs, and she took advantage of any booze left behind by the patrons. "I want to always have meth and never run out."

"You want to be a dealer?" She laughed at me.

"How much do you think I would need to start selling?"

"I'm not sure, come over after work and talk to my boyfriend about it."

So, after work I went straight to her place and met with Adam. "My tax return is coming and I want to start selling drugs," I told him.

Adam laughed at me too. "Why?"

"Because I want a constant supply and that seems like the best way to do it, but I don't know how."

"Well, it depends on how much money you have. You can take an 8 ball, break it down into quarters, sell enough quarters to replenish your supply, then do it all over again, as long as you can avoid using all your product."

My confusion must have been pretty obvious, either that or he was a psychic. He just laughed, pulled out a scale and some drugs. Then he gave me a crash course in methamphetamine dealing. He went on for hours about cutting the meth. "Don't use laxatives, people hate that shit. Sometimes people like vitamins that give you a rush of heat." He chopped up lines of meth cut with Niacin and we all snorted.

"Wow, that is the coolest sensation ever."

"Also, do not ever charge $25 for a quarter that only weighs ¼ of a gram – you should only charge $20 for that weight. If it weighs over, then bump up the price accordingly," he explained as he did a demonstration for me on the scale, "and don't sell dime bags."

Adam went on and on for hours in his crash course in the modern tactics of slinging methamphetamine. I absorbed everything like a sponge.

Tax return came. Check!

8-Ball purchased. Check!

Scale purchased. Check!

I decided I would be an ethical drug dealer so I skipped picking up any cut.

Adam forgot to tell me how to get customers and no business can stay afloat without them; so the early days of drug dealing were tough going. Then one day Heather set me up on a blind date with Kevin. I'll never forget the way this guy looked at me when he picked me up, let's just say I knew I had him if I wanted him. Also, he looked like he just stepped out of a Calvin Kline magazine, so I wanted him, too.

He took me to a really nice dinner, it was the first legitimate date I could remember being on, with steak and all of the everything I could want. Then we went to his house. He had cocaine and I had methamphetamine. We combined our supplies and I did my first speed ball. I really wanted to get naked with him, cause he was so cute and took me on my first real date. So, when he leaned in for a kiss the rest was history. We became inseparable and it wasn't long until he invited me to live with him.

He had a huge house that he shared with his mother, but he was an equal homeowner – they had a great relationship and she was rarely around. He was a construction worker at an out of town site and I was still a housekeeper. I bought an 8-ball of meth and he bought an 8-ball of cocaine every week that we combined. Birthday presents consisted of drug paraphernalia. It was all a lot of fun until we started getting into a lot of arguments about the drug supply.

He came home from a long day at work, bitching at me about the drugs. "You're going through a lot, there's hardly any left for me."

I would smile at him and take off my clothes – it was effective. I really enjoyed him and I enjoyed the drugs too. Why couldn't we all just get along?

The day came when I didn't have enough money for my share of the drugs, and I needed him to buy both. "No, you're using too much."

I couldn't believe he said no. "Are you fucking kidding me?"

"No, I'm not kidding, we need to cool off for a little while, and take a break." I waited for him to head out to work, then I went out and found a friend that could hook me up. Unfortunately, Kevin's mom found out what

44

I was doing, assumed I was dating someone else and Kevin broke up with me. "You're gonna need to move out, we'll give you a couple of months to find a new place to live, and you can have my room until you do."

I was really kind of sad about the break up but proceeded to date my friend as I tried to figure out what I was going to do next. He was hooking me up with some new meth that came into town and I hadn't slept in a very long time. I was sitting on the toilet when I saw a small bug, on its back, struggling to flip itself over. I decided to help the bug, so I grabbed a small piece of toilet paper and held it over the bug – waiting for the bug to grab onto it.

While waiting for the bug to grab on I noticed that there was actually a large spider web in the corner, and the bug was caught up in it. Then I saw that the spider web was actually HUGE and spanned the entire back corner of the bathroom. I jumped up off of the toilet and backed out of the bathroom slowly, visually scanning the room for the web's inhabitant – then I saw it!

A HUGE red and green daddy long leg, it was monstrous, and had colors like I had never seen on a spider, or on any insect for that matter. She started coming after me for trying to help her dinner escape. I was shocked, running backwards to get away, I could not believe my eyes. Then, I was shocked to be saved by these tiny little people who literally stepped out of the bathroom door, ripped her to pieces and ate her.

That spider screamed like nobody's business as these little wooden door people were eating her. Then they all waved at me, and spoke to me as they stepped back into the door and resumed their position. I kept looking at the bathroom, looking at the door, looking at the floor, in shock. Then I looked at the floor again and saw maggots. A whole bunch of them, all over the floor and on my feet.

That was when my shock and dismay was replaced with the screaming. I jumped up and down trying to get them off of my feet while screaming louder than I have ever screamed in my life. Kevin's mom ran to me calling 911, screaming with me, "What happened!?! What happened?"

I pointed around as I tried to tell her, "Look! There was a spider! She came from that web! Look at the maggots!"

She looked at everything. "There aren't any maggots anywhere!" She walked through the web in the bathroom. "What spider web?"

I grabbed her arm, pulled her to safety and pointed back down at the maggots again. "Look!" As I pointed at the maggots the floor suddenly morphed into the normal carpet again. It was a two-toned shaggy carpet so I could still see an imprint of where they were. I looked at the door again. "There were people!" I could see the outlines in the wood carved door of the people who stepped out.

"Sweetie," she said as she gently held my arm, "come sit down on the couch." We walked over and sat on the couch together. "What kind of drugs have you been using?"

I broke down and cried on her shoulder. I was really confused. I was embarrassed to say that the entire experience really happened to me. It was all very real, and I never once thought that it was a hallucination. I was afraid, I didn't understand it. I could not accept that it was methamphetamine's fault, so I chalked it up to cut.

"I really saw it," was the only answer I gave her.

"June, I don't want drugs in my house, I'm gonna need you to find somewhere else to live as soon as possible. For now, why don't you go get some rest?"

I followed her advice and laid down. As I passed by the bathroom I could still see the outline of those people who came out from the bottom of the door. I inched my way into the bathroom, I was nervous, but I confirmed there was no spider web. I checked for the little bug that started it all, it was a small piece of wood that must have broken off of a baseboard or something. I went to my room and passed out having been up for several days straight already; I was absolutely exhausted.

Several days later I was at work, and I moved a bed so I could get the sheets tucked in properly. I keeled over with a horrible stabbing pain in my stomach. Kevin was nice enough to come and pick me up from work – as I still did not have a license or a car. He took me home and I had to change clothes because of the bleeding. Kevin's mom gave me a muscle relaxant. I rested on the couch and his mother came to talk with me. "Do you think you might be pregnant?"

"Um, I don't know, I don't think so."

"When was your last period?"

"I stopped getting periods a couple of years ago from the birth control pills."

"How else have you been feeling? Tenderness in your breasts? Peeing a lot?"

"Actually, I peed my pants a couple of weeks ago, walking home from the store, I just couldn't hold it. It was kinda embarrassing." I laughed at myself, awkwardly.

"Let's take you down to get checked out."

"Ok."

We went down to a women's health clinic. Sadly enough, I was roughly 2-3 months pregnant and had just had the early stages of a miscarriage. Since I hadn't seen any large clots come out they weren't certain it was a full miscarriage and told me the process may have been interrupted by the muscle relaxants. I was given options. I could go through the process of abortion to ensure the pregnancy was terminated, or I could wait to see if I was still pregnant. If I waited, it would be too late to choose. "If you have been using drugs as frequently as you say, you probably did lose the baby. If you didn't lose the baby, the odds of carrying a healthy baby to term are very low."

I had never been ok with those moms out there who used drugs all throughout their pregnancies, then continued to drag their kids around to parties and such. It's not fair to the kids. At the same time, the thought of not being alone anymore was really intriguing.

Imagine a life in which there was a person who loved me unconditionally? It was a selfish act based in pure loneliness when I made my decision. "I will wait and see."

Eight

Sounds of Silence

⚜

*S*ounds of Silence
    Yesterday's sun that caressed and nurtured life was but a distant memory lost.
A storm of despair and fear was conceived in fury.
As I prepared for the sounds of silence.
(The Sounds of Silence, Jack Henslee)

Kevin's mother wasn't too crazy about my idea to try and keep the baby – if I was still pregnant. Kevin wouldn't speak on it at all, other than to tell me it was my choice. Kevin and I still had something, I would see it in his eyes when he looked at me, it was as if he regretted the decision to break up, but I had a new boyfriend that I was really excited about and was using Kevin for a place to live.

It's not that I didn't care about Kevin, because I did. But it was hard for me to truly care about anyone anymore, chalk it up to the life I had lived up to that point. I knew that in this world I was the only person who was going to look out for me. I suspected that Kevin and his mother might be a rare case, that they actually might care about me too. I only suspected it but wouldn't place any wager of hope on it, then, of course, she proved what I

48

instinctually knew to be true.

"June, I have decided that if you allow me to pay for an abortion, I will allow you to live here at the house. If you decide to keep the pregnancy, then I need you to leave, today."

I felt a ping of sadness. "How long do I have to decide?"

"Well, we all know the decision has to be made immediately, so, a few days."

Without saying another word I just got up, left the house and went for a walk. She had just proven what I already knew to be true. The one place I felt safe, the one place I felt loved, and they did not care at all about me. I was eager to find out what Kevin thought but he had been distant, physically distant, and I hadn't seen him in days.

I went to visit my ex-boyfriend Steve. I remember the night I connected with him, I was talking with him through the window of his tricked-out van. I had no idea he was paralyzed from the waist down until he got out of his van. It didn't deter me, I thought he was really cute and I have never been the kind of person to judge people externally. Having sex with a paraplegic was a lot more interesting than one might expect. We dated for months, and always remained friends. He was a shoulder to lean on, someone that would never hurt me. A safe person to go to talk with about my life, stuff I had been through, and major decisions I needed to make. I am not sure how he got so wise at such a young age but it's probably because he was not born paralyzed. It was a result of a gun-related tragedy that happened to him when he was young, but not too young to remember what life was like when he could walk. "Hey, June, how's it going?"

"Can I come in and hang out for a while?"

"No, my parents are home, but we can hang out front."

Steve wheeled out of the house and onto the lawn. I sat on the grass next to him. "How are you doing? I've been really worried about you."

"Why?"

"The last time I saw you I had to call an ambulance, something about being raped."

"Oh. I don't remember seeing you that night."

"You were pretty wasted."

"Well, I've been fine. Living with Kevin Bailey."

"Yeah, I heard."

"Everything in my life is about to change, finally."

"How so?"

"I'm pregnant."

Steve looked at me in the most condescending way a person can look at someone, it actually made me recoil a bit from the daggers shooting out of his eyes. "You can't seriously be thinking of having the baby."

"Yes!" I got up and crossed my arms in some strange gesture of defensive authority.

"June, you have no right to carry a baby."

"Who in the hell are you to tell me that?"

"You party way too much to be a mother."

"I'll stop."

Steve laughed at me. "Ok, so you're going to stop using everything for the next nine months, then stay home after you have the baby?" he asked in the most condescending way.

He made a good point, I don't think I ever thought of the length of a pregnancy. "Yes, asshole."

"How are you gonna take care of it?"

I shrugged my shoulders. "What do you mean?"

"You gonna make Kevin do all of that? I can't believe you're doing this. I thought you were cool."

"I can't believe what you're saying to me."

"June! You can't even take care of yourself! You have no right to bring a child into this world! Imagine the life that kid will have! It'll probably be deformed and made fun of its ENTIRE LIFE!"

He really pissed me off. I stormed off without saying another word to him as he turned his wheelchair and headed back into his house.

As unexpected and cold as they were, his words resonated with me. I had never thought of the gravity of the situation. That was a long time to go without any mind-altering substances, and then what? I was homeless, I had never lived on my own, I probably lost the baby anyways because of all of the drugs I was using.

What if the baby was deformed? What if my drug use had caused some horrible condition for the baby that the baby would have to live with his entire life? This is of course coming from someone permanently disabled and clearly miserable about it. Was I even ready to give up the drugs? I thought I could in exchange for a real-life partner.

I hadn't used in a couple of days and it was starting to gnaw at me, which is pretty much the reason I went to visit Steve. Now that Steve had scolded me all I could think of was getting high.

It was something about Steve, maybe it was the length of my relationship with him, or maybe it was because he was a person who had never harmed me in any way. But I just trusted what he said and I felt a really desperate need for his approval and his friendship. Every single word he said continued to resonate within me.

I walked for hours in confusion, then decided that since I was a worthless failure who would never amount to anything, I had no right to bring a child into the world. I would have the abortion, then hitchhike out of this god-forsaken hellhole and begin a new a life somewhere else. Where nobody knew me or the failures that I was running from.

Kevin's mother promised me that she would take me to the clinic, pay for the procedure, take care of me and let me stay as long as I needed. We did it. I'll never forget the people standing outside of the clinic with the horrible photos of aborted babies and the signs about pro-life. They made it awkward to go inside and do what needed to be done. It was also awkward leaving and wondering if they would be shouting at me, or throwing stones. I stared at them wondering if they really understood the various reasons that drove a woman into a clinic like that? Or if they think every baby should be carried to term, even if it had been exposed to epic quantities of drugs, every day, since the moment of conception?

After the clinic, we returned to the house and I was recovering on the couch – where Kevin's mother had relocated me. Kevin came home, sat down next to me and cried. That was the first moment I knew how Kevin felt about the pregnancy and that his views were drastically different from his mother's. There was a large part of me that knew the abortion was a waste of money and time. The baby died the day I had the cramping. There was no way that pregnancy was going to succeed. It was yet another manifestation of the failure of me.

Nine

All The World's A Stage

The deepest scars in life rest just beneath the surface.
The scars of regret.
The scars of disconnection.
The scars of an uncaring and selfish world.
The scars of being a woman in a world with no regard for a human being.
A world where women are merely objects.
As Shakespeare said, "All the world's a stage and all the men and women are merely players."
But we are not actors, we are human beings,
each day trying to find our footing on an unsteady terrain.

I left the house and started walking down the dark sidewalk. Although I was trying to not let it all bother me too much, I cried, very quietly, wondering where to go. I wanted to leave town but I wasn't sure where I wanted to go or how I would get there. I didn't have any money and I was leery of getting myself into the kind of trouble I'd got into in the past. I pondered my options as I walked down the street towards a gas station, trying to think of a safe acquaintance to call.

I spotted a group of guys across the street, there were five or six of them.

They spotted me too and called out to me, "Hey, lady, come over here and talk." I acted like I didn't hear or see them as I picked up the pace. "Hey!" they yelled. I watched them out of the corner of my eye as they started looking for a break in the cars so they could cross the street to where I was. I hustled faster, trying to be discreet, because running from a pack of wolves immediately speaks to their cardinal instinct to chase but my discretion didn't work.

They started running full speed across the street towards me. I turned and ran, as fast as I could too. I was heading straight for the gas station across the street as I zig zagged my way through the obstacle course of cars – which was the only thing that slowed them down. Once inside the gas station they caught up quick but stayed outside of the front doors, pacing.

I ran straight to the clerk. "I need to use your phone please."

He looked at me, then he looked at my pursuers lingering outside the front doors. "They with you?"

"They were chasing me! Call the police!"

He visually scanned them, as if he was assessing the situation somehow, then looked back at me.

"No."

"What?"

"I not get involved."

"Please! They're chasing me."

The clerk ignored me and resumed organizing the area behind his counter. He nodded over to the front doors. "You need to leave unless you are paying customer."

"You are a disgusting sack of shit! I'm staying. You want me gone? Call the police and they can make me leave." I could see the men pacing back and forth in front of the store, one was staring at me, looking very disappointed that I was inside. I stepped up to the counter. "What the hell is wrong with you?"

"They shoot up my store if I get involved."

"Will you at least call a friend of mine?"

He shook his head at me.

"Then it looks like I'm staying for a while."

I hung out in the corner of the store and the guys eventually walked out of view. I didn't trust that they had simply given up and left, so I remained posted inside. The clerk finally offered to call one of my friends for me, but refused to call the police. I had him call Howard, I knew he lived close by so it wouldn't take him long to pick me up. He pulled as close to the front doors as possible. Once outside I could see the guys that had chased me, they had moved on to chasing someone else.

Howard was a close friend of my aunt. I met him while I was living with her and he always told me that if I ever needed anything, anything at all, to call him.

"What's going on?"

"Those guys were chasing me and that guy at the gas station wouldn't call the cops."

"So, where do you need a ride to?"

"I need a place to stay. I was thinking of my aunt's house."

"I don't think she's home, and I'm not sure she wants you there."

"Can I sleep on your couch tonight?"

"Sure."

Howard lived in a tiny little one-bedroom apartment. He cleaned the place up a little and handed me bedding to make up the couch for myself. I stayed for several days while pondering what my next move should be. It was a much-needed rest considering all that I had recently been through. He handed me a TV dinner. "So, have you figured out what you want to do?"

"I think I wanna go back to Talutha."

"Back?" Howard said as he knocked back a beer. He nodded the bottle at me.. "Want one?"

"No, I don't drink anymore." I went into his kitchen and got myself a soda. Then returned to the couch that had become my new home. "I was there when I was in foster care. It's a small, quiet town – I really want a fresh start. I've burned too many bridges around here."

"Yeah, I can't disagree with you there. How far is this place?"

"Pretty far. I really need a bus ticket."

"You got someone to stay with when you get there?"

"No, but I had friends in high school and the counselors from foster care."

"June, I need to ask you a favor."

"What's that?"

"I was wondering if you'll take my picture for me."

"Sure, where's the camera?"

"It's in my bedroom, hold on." Howard disappeared into his bedroom. I stayed on the couch, staring at the TV but not paying a lot of attention. Then I heard him calling for me. "Come in to my bedroom." I thought the situation seemed a little strange but he'd been great so far. So, I walked to his bedroom, stepped in, and saw something I knew I would never be able to unsee. Howard, the old man Howard, was sprawled out on his bed, completely naked.

"Whoa!" I said as I covered my eyes and spun around. "What the fuck?" I headed straight for the front door, stopping long enough to grab my things and put on my shoes.

"Wait!" he yelled as he ran out of his room, wrapped in a blanket, "Where are you going? I thought you said you would take my picture?"

"Um, naked? Naked? I don't want to know what you look like naked. You're a freak!" He stepped towards me and I picked up a lamp. "Stay the fuck away from me. I can totally take your old perverted ass."

"It's not like I asked you to touch me, I just, I needed the photos!" Howard backed up slowly. "Please, don't, just let me explain myself."

"EXPLAIN!" I charged at him a couple of steps, "and give me all the money in your wallet!" I charged at him a little more. "It's payment for my burning eyes!"

"Let me go put my clothes on."

"No! You stay where I can see you."

"I am not a pervert."

"Yes, you fucking are!"

"Do you have any idea how hard it is to sleep at night knowing that you're out here on my couch? I have tried to behave myself and I just can't anymore." He shook his head, slumped down into his recliner and cried. "I am not a pervert. I just wanted you to take my picture because I wanted you to see me, to pay attention to me, look at all that I have done for you and I haven't touched you, not once. Please don't tell anyone. You can have all the money in my wallet and I'll put you up in a hotel room."

"Where's your wallet?"

"It's in my bedroom."

I went in and grabbed his wallet, there was hardly any money in it but I took what was there and left on foot. I walked to the nearest hotel and used his money to get a room. The next day I walked to the nearest fast food restaurant and got a job. I needed more nights in the hotel room so I made Howard come down and pay for it. He did, and then he quietly left. This was our arrangement for my promise to not tell my whole family that he was a pervert. I calculated minimum wage by hours and found out how much a bus ticket to Talutha would cost. When a fast food restaurant fires you, they have to pay you the same day, but if you quit you have to wait two weeks. So, I worked there for the exact number of hours I needed to pay for the bus ticket, then on the day I was ready to cash out I told my boss to fuck off. I had my check later that day, cashed it, went straight to the bus station and took the next bus out of town to Talutha County.

Ten

The Greener Grass

The grass is always greener on the other side, but when we get to the other side, we will always spot even greener grass on another side.

The bus ride to Talutha was a long one filled with excitement and fear of the unknown. I had the noblest of intentions, I was going to prove I was capable of taking care of myself. I was cleaning up my act. I would find a job right away and steer clear of all the parties. I felt like I needed to prove myself but I am not sure who I was proving myself to, since I was literally leaving everyone behind. I had not been to Talutha in years and I had no clue where anyone was, but I was done. Nobody in my life cared about me and I was done caring in return.

I almost immediately ran into old friends from the foster home that let me tag along. Humorous as it was, they were all homeless too. There were about six of us and we set up a camp underneath a bridge in town. We went to the local cruise on the weekends and all of the parties that followed. The irony of traveling miles just to find myself in the exact same situation I had just left behind was not lost on me.

Natia was living under the bridge with us and she became my closest friend. She had family in LA and daydreamed about getting a ride to them so that she could get off the streets.

"You and I should go to LA."

"What would we do there?"

Natia looked around the camp. "I'm pretty much thinking anything is better than here."

I laughed. "I used to be a singer. Maybe I could do that in LA?"

"Ooooh, that would be the best place."

"We could totally go. Let's find out how much a bus ticket is, then we can get jobs and go as soon as we have the money."

"Jobs? We can't get no jobs." She laughed at me. "You're kidding with me, right?" She kept laughing.

"Watch me," I said as I laughed back at her. "I'll go get a job at that little hot dog place tomorrow."

She laughed at me again like I had just told her a funny joke.

"I'm serious," I insisted.

The next day I went to the hot dog joint, slipped into their bathroom, bathed in their sink, made sure my clothing was presentable, then walked up to the counter and asked for an application. I was hired on the spot.

When I went home to our little concrete bungalow of joy under the stinky bridge and I showed off my new hot dog flipping ensemble, Natia laughed at me. "I can't believe you were serious! Look at you go."

"I'll be laughing at you too as soon as I see you in yours! Get in there tomorrow, let's get ourselves out of this shithole."

"Ok."

"Did you figure out how much the bus tickets are?"

"No, I was tired," she said.

"It can't be that expensive but I'm gonna go find out." I got up to walk to the bus station. "Wanna come?"

"Nah, I don't feel good."

"Alright, I'll be back."

I walked to the bus station, it wasn't very far from camp. I walked into the lobby and stared at the big bus schedule board for a long time. So many different places to go but the bus to LA was $36. I was supposed to be working 15 hours a week, minimum wage was $3.75, so by my calculations, one paycheck would get me to LA. I walked back to camp.

"Alright, you need $36 to get the ticket."

"No problem, I've got that already."

"Yes! You should go get a ticket."

"I'll wait for you so we can go together."

I should have seen the signs, it seemed like she wanted to go, it was her idea to go to LA, but the effort to make it happen seemed to be entirely absent. Meanwhile, I had my work cut out for me. Living under a bridge meant no shower or running water. I was able to sleep but it wasn't the best sleep in the world and the absence of a clock presented its own layer of complications too.

Bathing in the bathroom sink at work had become too awkward so I started using the sink in a fast food restaurant across the street. I think I pulled off my whole façade pretty well, I never got the impression that anyone at work had any idea I was a homeless girl bathing in public bathroom sinks. It was an exhausting juggling act and after two weeks I just couldn't keep it up anymore. By then I had what I needed so I pulled my traditional move and got myself fired so that I could get my check right away. I bought my bus ticket and went straight to Natia. I showed it to her so that she could get a ticket on the same bus.

"Great! I'll go get my ticket right now," she said and walked towards the bus station as I went and sat down at a restaurant to eat and drink a lot of soda. What I really wanted was a hotel room but after buying the bus ticket I couldn't afford one.

On the day of the bus departure I searched everywhere for her and finally found her at the last minute. She didn't have a ticket or any money to buy one. "You can go on ahead without me."

"How? I don't know any of your family. What the hell would I do when I got there?"

"You could give me your ticket and then get yourself another one?"

"But I don't have the job anymore."

"I'm sure you'll think of something."

I am not a total idiot, I knew what was happening here but I had absolutely nowhere to go in LA. I knew absolutely no one in LA and I suspected LA would chew me up and spit me out. I simply dreaded the idea of going it alone. The idea of a fresh start in LA was the inspiration that propelled me through the two weeks of living an act as I bathed in the sinks of public bathrooms. I drew my strength from the hope of a new life there and it was all I had thought about for weeks. I handed her my ticket. "Regardless of what happens, at least one of us won't be under the bridge anymore." I felt the death of hope strike deep as I handed over all of my hard work to my lazy side-kick.

Natia burst into tears. "Oh my God, you're serious?!?"

I smiled at her, I was on the verge of tears myself, but they fell from a different emotional well. "Take it."

Natia almost took me down with a hug.

"You better get to that bus station before you miss the bus, I'd hate for the money to go to waste."

She kissed me all over my face, then grabbed my arm and pulled me down the sidewalk with her. "Walk with me so we can make plans."

I gently pulled away from her, I didn't want to rain on her parade but I was not happy. Her moment of excitement only marked another personal failure for me, of epic proportions, and I had to step off because being around her was like bathing in it. "Na, I'm tired, I wanna go sit down."

"Well, let me give you my parents' number." She pulled a pen out of her pocket and wrote it on my hand. "Call me in a couple of days, you'll be able to come and live with me at my parents' house when you get down there. They're gonna love you for doing this for me!" She gave me another hug, then ran off with my hopes and dreams as I stood there feeling like the biggest sucker in the world.

She seemed sincere but I had a nagging feeling that I had been worked over pretty good. Of course, this type of nagging feeling was the norm for me anyways. But, how many times did my nagging feelings ring true? Almost every time. I didn't see this as some monumental gift of intuition. I didn't see this as something psychic. I saw this as a fact of life. People are liars, through and through. The reason my nagging feelings always rang true was because I had learned a thing or two about human nature. Lots of people say lots of things but rarely had I seen any of them actually live by the words falling out of their mouths.

In spite of my nagging feelings there was always a facet of me that hoped I was wrong. I really tried to make sure I never put stock in that layer of wishful thinking. It was like how it feels to hope that I get to go to Hawaii someday before I die. I hoped I would someday but I would never get my hopes up for it. That's about how much I allowed myself to entertain the idea that someone was being honest with me. Natia's parents' phone number was a lot like that hope of someday going to see Hawaii. Not because they were originally from Hawaii, but because getting someone to answer the phone was like trying to get a cruise to Hawaii while bathing in sinks and sleeping under a bridge.

I gave up on making a new life for myself. I went out and found the biggest meth dealer in town. He was too creepy to date but I definitely set out to be his best friend in the whole wide world, and nailed it. I rode around with him all over town as he was making his deliveries. He was from Hawaii too, coincidentally enough, and he claimed his product was from there too. I met the who's who in the Talutha Methamphetamine industry. It's one of those situations where, once you become a part of that world there isn't a whole lot of wiggle room for turning around and leaving. Especially when you're an 18-year-old homeless girl with no license, no car, no friends, and a bed that is made out of concrete, underneath a busy bridge.

I loved the meth world, because nobody sleeps, so nobody needs a place to lay their head down at night. Another great perk is that meth takes care of all of your nutritional needs too, I was never hungry. This is absolutely perfect for a homeless girl without a single cent to her name. There were no judgements, if I needed a shower I could just use one, so no more fast food restroom sponge baths either.

Sooner or later the party would always have to wind down. I never told anyone that I didn't have anywhere to go, I would just very casually go my own way and wander the streets – ironically enough it was just safer that way. One time I was coming down so hard I could barely keep my eyes open, so I went back to the old camp under the bridge.

I was hopeful some of my fellow campers were still around but it was a dark and deserted ghost town. I felt the darkness provided me the safe shelter I needed so I laid down, or should I say, fell down and was well on my way to passing out. I was startled by the rustling of nearby bushes, and suddenly my heart was pounding so loudly that it felt like I just did a fresh line of meth. "How's it going?" a male voice rang out from the darkness. I knew he couldn't know I was a woman, it was too dark under there for anyone to see anything. The only thing that could give me away was my voice.

I paused for a long time, terrified to expose the fact that I was a woman, alone under the bridge. Drawing on my years in choir I reached down for my lowest alto notes and said "good" sounding as much like a man as possible. I never, in my wildest dreams, expected all of my years singing in choir to become some type of a survival skill. Keeping in mind, this male voice had not done anything to me but I had been through too much to go on faith. In order to survive the streets, it is imperative to automatically assume the worst until you put yourself in a defensible location.

It seemed to work because he didn't say another word, but the awkward silence had me wondering if he was questioning my gender. Regardless of what he was thinking, I knew that I was crazy to think I could just pass out down there. If worst case scenario happened I would have zero chance of getting help, and limited options of self-defense. I had to get up and move. I waited for a little while to be casual about it and then worked my way out from under the bridge.

It really sucked, I was so exhausted I could hardly see straight and I had literally nowhere to go and get some rest. I sat on a bus bench for a long time, then laid down on it for a couple of minutes, till some men walked by trying to talk to me. I ignored them, got up and started walking like I had somewhere to go. This was always my act out there, I always made sure to look like I had somewhere to go. I felt too defenseless if I looked lost and confused. Always look like you're going somewhere, always carry yourself with confidence, do not look like a victim. It was a valuable lesson I picked up in my self-defense training, which later on became Shotokan Karate.

Later that night I ran into an old Indian dude I'd met in all of my homeless travels. The homeless world is a small world. You spend enough time on the streets and there's a certain camaraderie that develops. Some of the drunk bums sitting around begging for change are really awesome people who would literally give away their last cigarette or their last little bit of money to help another homeless person out of a jam. Or at least, to help an 18-year-old homeless female. He tipped me off to an abandoned house that people squat in. He also tipped me off to the fact that the post office is open all night and sometimes he goes in there to stay warm.

I walked to the house of squatters and got a really bad feeling in my stomach. The post office was within view of the house, it seemed very warm, welcoming, well-lit and safe. So, the post office took the win. Once inside I found a spot on the floor that was relatively concealed from the view of the front entrance. There was a little counter for filling out envelopes, I curled up on the floor underneath it, covered my face with my arm and passed out.

Day in and day out I passed the time hanging out at the mall. Sometimes I hung out at the mall in plain view. The mall was designed in a very unique way, they had these wooden structures that were up above certain walkways. They resembled tree houses and underneath them were these huge planters and wishing wells. Some of the structures had stairwells and mall goers had fun taking their kids up into the treehouse structures. Some of the structures were just for show and did not have stairwells. Being limber and somewhat acrobatic, I was able to use the planters below as a springboard to hoist myself up.

Once up there I sank right into the perfect hideout a person like me could ever ask for. It was quiet, and private. It felt like having my own private room again which was truly an indescribable feeling of relief. It became a regular outlet of escape from my mundane existence that I never told another living soul about.

I met Mike and Sue at the mall. We ran into each other as we were all three on the same mission – finding a cigarette. We got to talking and decided the best plan of action was to steal some from one of the stores inside of the mall. The security there was pretty top-notch, so it was best to take the place down as a team. We worked really well together and got our cigarettes. We got a lot more than cigarettes though, we all got a new friend. Who knew that the process of shoplifting would be such a great team building exercise?

Mike gave me a fist bump as we popped open a pack of smokes. "Where do you live?"

"Ah, here, there, and everywhere."

"Come on over and hang out at the motel anytime – I got a lot of other jobs I'm trying to do but I need a good assistant."

Sue came up, wrapped her arms around Mike and winked at me. "And I need a good three-some."

I laughed with her and Mike gave her a dirty look. "We don't do that shit anymore! Come over, the threesome she's talking about ain't what it sounds like."

I liked these two so I was all for it. "Let's go!" I followed them to the motel where they had a son, Michael, that was sleeping in the room by himself.

These two became my closest friends. We hung out just about every single day, scheming on new and inventive ways to get our hands on cash, food, cigarettes, and anything else we needed. I would never accept any of their food or sleep on their floor - it was a golden rule of mine. I had burned too many bridges in my previous town to let myself do it again here. Their friendship was too valuable to me and I worried that if I spent too much time at their place I would ruin it – like I felt I had ruined every other relationship that had any value in my life.

I suppose I had simply grown to recognize and appreciate new relationships that I wanted to hold onto. I was also picky about jobs that we did, it always had to be for the right reason and I would only shoplift from major chains that I knew had insurance. I just had some weird notions about Karma. I truly believed that in Karmic law it was ok to steal from a huge retailer but it wasn't ok to steal from a privately-owned mom and pop store.

I adamantly believed that food should be free, I was adamantly against the government, and I despised major for-profit organizations. I also wasn't crazy about churches that looked so elaborate that they clearly had a lot of money coming in. I looked down on them in a very harsh way as I felt that their sole purpose was to trick people into thinking they cared, when all they wanted was to tap deeply into the hearts of many, to trick them into reaching deep into their pockets when the basket came around the room. I thought they all had it coming and needed to learn a lesson.

In any case, we hung out pretty regularly coming up with strategies to get us by and on the weekends, I would go back to the cruise, follow the parties to the after parties, more after parties, then hang out for as many days as it seemed natural, which usually meant hooking up with some guy I met at one of the parties. I'd be there sleeping with him for a couple of days, sometimes a week. I never stayed in the same place for too long before going back to my usual routine, and eventually showing back up at the motel. They looked forward to hearing my stories because they didn't get out a lot.

My life was a sack of shit but it worked, I had a system, and the post office floor was safe. I was laying in my usual spot when I heard the police radio. I tried to pretend I couldn't hear anything, hoping they were there for something else, worried that something terrible had happened. "Excuse me, ma'am?" Someone was touching my shoulder. "Are you ok?"

I rolled over to see flashes of red and blue reflecting off several pairs of shiny black shoes. Then I looked up to meet the gaze of the firemen, EMT's and a couple of cops. An EMT was kneeling down beside me while one of the cops shined a flashlight on me, scanning my face and body. "How are you feeling?"

"Fine."

The cop manning the flashlight spoke up. "We got a disturbance call that you were injured here in the post office, is that true?"

"Uh, no." I sat up, confused. "What happened? Who called?"

The cop turned off his flashlight. "You been drinking tonight?"

"No, what the hell is going on here? I was sleeping." I yawned. "And well, too, till you guys came along."

The cop seemed about as annoyed as me, but I didn't understand why.

66

It's not like he had just been rudely awoken from a good night's sleep and I really wanted to know who the asshole was that called "who's the asshole that called you guys? Cause they're making shit up."

"They were concerned about you." He pointed around at the rescue workers. "Hence the cavalry," he said to me with a sarcastic scowl. "Why the hell are you in the post office?"

I glanced down at his nametag, D. Corbin. "What kinda cop are you?"

"You are really trying my patience here." He took a deep breath as if he was trying to calm his temper as his face turned a little red. "I'm Deputy Sheriff Corbin." He pointed at his nametag. "Can you stand up for me please?"

"Yes." I got up onto my feet, and the EMT stood up with me. "I was just, really tired and I didn't have anywhere to go."

It was obvious Deputy Corbin didn't believe me. "So you just thought it was ok to sleep on the floor of the post office, huh?" Corbin nodded to the EMT. "What do you think?"

The EMT looked at me. "You sure you're ok?" he asked, then looked at Corbin. "She seems ok to me." He nodded at the firemen, then back at me. "If you don't need our help we can go."

Corbin started shining his flashlight in my eyes again.

"God, you guys, yes! I was sleeping!"

Corbin stepped in closer and yelled at me, "You stop shouting at these guys, they're just trying to do their job!" He turned to the EMT. "You guys can get going, thank you for your service." Then Corbin returned his attention to me. "Look into this flashlight."

Frustrated and tired, I shut up and cooperated with the sobriety test. I stared at the flashlight while he checked my pupils, then he put away his flashlight, pulled out a notepad, and started asking a bunch of questions. "What's your name?"

"June."

"June?" He stared at me in agitation.

"Taylor."

"Date of Birth?"

"November 8, 1969."

"Show me some ID."

"Shit, I don't have any," I said.

He lowered the pen and notepad as if wondering what to do with me.

"What kind of drugs you been using tonight?"

"None, I swear."

"Well, I'm having a real hard time believing you and you're gonna have to show me some kind of ID."

I dug through my stuff and found something with my name on it to show him. Then, as if a miracle was sent down from heaven he got a call from Dispatch for something way more serious than little old me. "I guess it's your lucky day cause I gotta go. But do not let me catch you sleeping here anymore, got it?"

I nodded at him.

"Come on and walk out with me."

I followed him to the door, he opened it and waved for me to go through first as he lectured me. "It's illegal and I could bust you for trespassing. You want that?"

By now we were outside and walking down the front steps as he hustled to his patrol car; he looked back at me. "Well do ya?"

I quietly shook my head.

"Consider yourself warned, waste our time like this again and you ARE going to jail," he promised as he hopped in his car and sped away.

Luckily, the sun was rising. One door of the mall was already open for the very early morning mall walkers. I went in acting like I was one of them. My painstaking efforts to blend in didn't seem to be working though, as evidenced by all the scowling senior citizens. It must have been my attire, I was fresh out of hot pink jumpsuits.

Eleven

Doughnuts

I wandered all night with nowhere to go, sitting on bus benches again, till I finally went back to the Post Office. I got through the night and in the morning, I awoke to a surprise gift on the table above me. Someone had left me doughnuts and milk. I looked around but there was no one to be found. I took the gift and scarfed it down. The next night I woke up to Deputy Corbin standing over me again. "You are not supposed to be here, you know this. It brings me no joy to do this but I am arresting you for trespassing," and he motioned with his hands, "get up." I got up. "You got some proper ID now?" I shook my head. "Full name."

"June Taylor."

He used his shoulder mic to tell my name to dispatch. "Date of birth?"

"November 8."

"Year?"

"1969."

He gave the information to dispatch. "Since you can't seem to find another place to sleep, I'm gonna help you out and put you somewhere safe."

"Oh my God, thank you." I smiled in relief.

Then he pulled out his handcuffs. "Turn around."

I cried, "What? Why?"

"Just turn around."

He handcuffed me, walked me to his car, put me in the back seat and drove to the jail.

"You don't understand, I just don't have anywhere else to go and I don't want to sleep on a bus bench. The Post Office is the safest place I have."

"Well, you'll be in a much safer place now, hell they'll even feed you."

I laid my head down on the back seat and closed my eyes. "By the way, thank you."

"You're going to jail, no matter how cute you try to be."

"I mean, thank you for the doughnuts and milk." He ignored me as he turned up his radio – but I knew it was him.

I was in jail for a few days till they cut me loose at my arraignment, there weren't any charges filed against me. I was released on a Friday, perfect timing for the cruise. That night I met someone amazing, Ryan. One of the nicest people I had ever met in my life. I told him about the post office and my little jail ordeal and he invited me to come and stay at his trailer with him. He was soooooo genuine and nice, he was like a child but was at least in his 30s. He was definitely a 13-year-old in a 30-year-old body. He was mentally disabled and completely self-supporting through his disability income. "My home is your home," he said to me as we stepped into his super tiny trailer.

The bathroom was like an outhouse, there was no running water, there was hardly any room to walk around due to his dirty laundry and trash. There were two twin beds and he gave one of them to me. Sometimes instinct just tells us about a person, and this person I knew would never hurt a fly. He was truly just looking for a platonic friend to party with. If he had any sexual interest in me he would have been too shy and immature to say it or try anything. It was a PERFECT situation for both of us because I would never hurt him either.

We both went to the cruise on the weekends and partied with a lot people in between. Then one day we met Bob. He seemed cool, he came to the trailer and hung out a lot. He told us a sad story of woe, "You guys should help me get my truck, my aunt took it and they won't give it back."

I rooted for him. "Screw that, if it's your truck it's your truck."

"Listen, guys, I own a bunch of cars. I'll give one to both of you if you can just help me get them back from my family."

Ryan finally spoke up, "I don't need a car, I don't even know how to drive."

I moved over and sat next to Bob. "I don't know either but I would love to have a car." I was really excited. Having a car meant finally having a place of my own. I loved hanging with Ryan but the weather had gotten hot. Many long, boring, hot days were spent in that trailer. Blisteringly hot. Blistering to the point of tacky skin. This was bad enough as it was, but there were also flies, lots, and lots, of flies. For countless days, I'd lay there in the blistering heat, trying to sleep as the flies landed on my nose – imagining I was a mere carcass, baking in the hot desert as vultures circled above me. I'd try to find some relief in the daydream of leaving the sweatbox of a trailer, to go sit in the shade somewhere. I pitched it to Ryan but his energy was picked clear to the bone, his lack of enthusiasm was met by mine.

It's taxing to be a carcass, but a car sounded like a breath of fresh air, especially if it had an air conditioner. "Let's do it!! Where do we go? How fast can we get it?"

Bob laughed at me. "Today, let me go get my things and I'll come back to pick you up later."

As soon as he left Ryan moved over next to me. "I don't have a good feeling about this at all."

"What? What do you mean?"

"This doesn't make any sense, that's what I mean."

"He's solid, man, he's just trying to hook us up if we help him."

"I don't think we should."

I wrapped my arms around him. "Pleeeeeeeeeease!"

"Ok, if you want me to help I will. But you're not bringing any of the cars back here to the trailer."

"Why?"

"Cause they're probably stolen and my parents would get pissed at me. As it is they're asking why I have someone living out here with me, this is technically their property."

"Ok, when he gives me the car we'll put it in the park."

"Perfect."

A few hours later Ryan returned in a new truck. "You guys ready?"

Excited, I ran out to the truck, Ryan came quietly, clearly not approving of what we were doing. Bob drove us quite a way into the mountains and eventually pulled into the driveway of a secluded house, Ryan suspicious, and I was kinda wondering what was going on too. Ryan was the first to question him, "This isn't a wrecking yard, and I don't see any cars around here."

Bob winked at us. "Relax, man, this is my aunt's house. I had to come here first to get the keys, then we'll go over to the shop that they're holding the cars in. Oh, and the one I'm giving you is in the garage here."

I happily waited in the truck with Ryan who seemed pretty antsy. When Bob returned he was carrying a television, and a bunch of other stuff. Ryan just shook his head, looked down at the floorboard and muttered "I didn't see anything."

Bob hopped back into the truck. "What?" Bob shut the door and fired up the engine. "That's all my stuff."

Ryan replied, "Sure it is, man."

I didn't care whose stuff it was, I was just giddy about my new car that I was expecting to see at any moment now. I leaned over Ryan to smile at Bob. "Did you get the keys? Where's the car?" Bob met my smile as he pulled a bunch of keys out of his pocket then drove away from the house "what about the car?

"I'll bring it to you later, I gotta go do something else right now, I'm taking you guys home."

I was really disappointed and immediately started wondering if I, we, had done something wrong? He never said he needed our help inside of the house and it really just seemed kind of weird that he had us tag along if we weren't going to go inside. It was probably because of all of Ryan's little comments, maybe he thought we weren't cool? As he pulled up to Ryan's trailer I was struggling to contain my disappointment but I didn't want to come off rude and ungrateful so I just quietly hopped out of the truck. Ryan slid out behind me, and as I closed the door Bob pulled away. Then he stopped, backed up to us, rolled down the window and said, "I'll be back later with the car, then around midnight we'll go to the yard for the rest of them."

Once inside Ryan's sweatbox of a trailer, he jumped in the air, clapped his heels together, and shouted, "Woo! Hoo! We're accessories!"

I was kind of agitated and grieving about my unrealized dreams of getting the free car. I flopped down onto my bed, sacrificing myself up to the vultures as I stared at the old, dingy and depressing trailer ceiling. "We didn't do anything."

A few hours later Bob actually came back. "Where do you want me to put the car?"

"Yes!" I jumped off of the bed and raced out of the trailer to see he was towing an old, beat up Toyota Corolla. It was covered in dirt, spider webs and clearly hadn't been cared for in years.

"It doesn't run, but all it needs is a tune up. You know how to do that?"

"No, but I'll find someone."

"Alright, where do you want me to park it?"

"Let's take it to the park, it's just a couple of blocks away."

"Sounds good, show me where."

We hopped into the truck and I directed him to the nearby park. There was a huge oak tree providing a beautiful area of shade, it was a true sight for sore eyes, or should I say anyone who had been suffering in the blistering heat of a trailer with no air conditioning. I didn't care if this thing ran or not, the shady parking spot promised to be my new oasis, it truly is the little things sometimes.

I gave Bob such a huge hug I just about knocked him over, he said, "I'll help you get this running soon, but I gotta go for now, but I'll be back later so you can help me out with the others. I need you to drive a car out of my aunt's shop, but we gotta wait till after midnight."

I shook his hand. "Deal!"

Then he took off and I got into the car. I rolled down the windows and enjoyed the shady breeze. There were some cobwebs inside, but I didn't care, I was having a warm and fuzzy moment. It was the first time anyone had ever given me anything so awesome. He didn't try to get my clothes off or anything. The kindness absolutely blew me away, I cried, tears of joy. I was too excited to see that I was acting very gullible. Me, the one who had been hardened throughout the young years of my life. Me, who trusted no one. I guess I was just too excited to see the truth of the situation, if it's too good to be true that's because it is. Dummy me.

A little while later Ryan walked up. "Wow, so he really just gave this to you, huh?"

"In exchange for a favor, he'll be back later."

"Let's fire it up, I wanna go to the store."

"It doesn't run, he said it just needs new spark plugs."

"I know a guy that works on cars, he was in jail for a while but I heard he just got out. Let's walk over to his house."

"Yes!"

We walked to Ryan's friend's house and he introduced me to Matt. I had a little bit of meth on me so I offered Matt a line and told him about the car. Matt was totally willing to help. We all set out on foot to walk back over to the park when Bob showed back up in the truck. Ryan recoiled. "I don't wanna go with you."

"Why?"

"You know why, June, you guys go, come pick me up when Bob's gone."

I shrugged my shoulders at him. "OK."

Matt and I hopped into the truck. As we approached the car we saw some guys parked nearby. They were standing outside of their truck, leaning over the hood. As soon as Bob saw them he gunned the truck we were in. The other guys hopped into their truck and pursued us. I yelled, "Let us out!!" Bob just drove faster as he rolled down his window and threw all of the car keys out into a field. I screamed at him, "Who are those guys!" Bob ignored me and floored the gas. "Let us out!" Bob laughed at me and kept flooring it as the other guys chased. Bob turned down a very steep hill, started down the hill and then opened the door and jumped out of the truck. He was gone.

The truck was careening down the hill with no driver. Matt started screaming, "Grab the wheel!"

I grabbed it but it was really hard to turn. I screamed, "I can't!" as I wrestled with the steering wheel and tried get into the driver's seat. The truck was completely out of control and headed for another truck at a really fast speed. Matt leapt over me and grabbed the steering wheel. By then I was finally in the driver's seat, and I slammed on the breaks. I jumped out of the truck and took off running as I heard the pursuing truck slam into ours. I ran, and ran, and ran into the shadows. I was hiding behind a tree as I watched them yank Matt out of the truck and start shaking him around like a rag doll.

And here I go again. I cared. I didn't even know this guy but I seem to have been born with this inherent need to help others. I seemed to have been born with this inherent need to accept responsibility for my actions. It was stupid. I was stupid. I needed to pay for trusting Bob. I needed to pay for my actions. I had to be punished, not Matt. I walked back down there. "Hold on! Let him go! He didn't do anything wrong. The guy you're looking for ran off that way." I pointed in the direction he ran.

One of the men yelled and slapped the truck we just got out of, "This is my truck!"

I tried to be as polite to these guys as possible, "We were riding with a friend, he said this was HIS truck. I had no idea it was stolen from any." I barely finished the last word of my sentence as my mouth fell silent at the sight of the Sheriff's patrol car pulling up. I could feel my heart actually sink into my toes at the sight of Deputy Corbin stepping out of the car.

Of course, it had to be him. Out of all the cops in the area, it was him. I mean really? Him? Why couldn't be a different cop? I was kind of embarrassed and awkwardly grasping for a conversation starter when I blurted out, "I'm not sleeping in the post office anymore." He kinda glared at me, I guess he didn't think it is was funny. I could feel everyone else looking at me too and I stood there wishing I had just kept my mouth shut. It was only a momentary lapse, as I quickly resumed my attitude of world hatred.

"June, of course." He nodded to the men for answers. "What's she been up to tonight?" It was clear I had zero chance of getting out of this one and the shitty part was – I technically did nothing wrong.

One of the men dragged Matt over to him by the collar. "They stole my truck!"

Corbin nodded to the truck. "This here's your truck?"

"Yeah." The man let go of Matt's collar as he kind of shoved him into Corbin's reach.

"Why don't you take a seat in my car while I sort this out."

Matt nodded his head. "I don't want any trouble, man, I didn't steal anything! I don't even know these people!"

"Alright, you got ID on you?"

Matt nodded again. "It's in my back pocket."

"Got any weapons on you?"

"Nah, man."

"Alright, gimme your wallet." Matt slowly pulled out his wallet and handed it to Corbin. He followed Corbin over to the patrol car, Corbin opened the door and Matt cooperatively sat down. "Just cool off here for a few while I sort this out and then I'll get your statement." Corbin turned to his radio and called dispatch for back up.

I walked over to Corbin. "Matt's telling the truth! We didn't steal the truck! It was Bob, he stole the truck!" I pointed to where Bob ran.

Corbin smiled at me. "Who the hell is Bob?"

"This guy, he was giving us a ride. When these other guys started chasing us he jumped out of the truck and ran off into that field over there! I'm telling you, he's probably still over there! He's the one you should be talking to!" I started to realize I was wasting my breath as Corbin's smile indicated that he found what I was saying to be very, um, entertaining. Soon he was laughing with the backup who came, and of course the men who were chasing us. This was like one of the rare moments I was telling the truth but nobody would believe me.

As Corbin put the handcuffs on me he gave me a little lecture. "Well, June, you graduated from Trespassing to Grand Theft Auto. What kinda trouble are you aiming for next?"

It was Thursday so I got to spend my whole weekend in jail. It sucked but there was air conditioning at least. It was the first night of peaceful sleep that I had in a long, long, time. I was laying there flat on my stomach, falling asleep in the dark cell, alone. Completely alone, when I heard a voice whisper, "June!" into my ear. It was more than just hearing the whisper, I actually felt the breath move my hair. I catapulted off of that bed in a way I had never moved before. I looked around the dark cell, and nobody was there. It took a while to calm myself down but eventually I laid back down.

I was walking through a grassy meadow, with a beautiful river flowing nearby. I sat on the edge of the river, amidst a meadow filled with beautiful wild Orchids, Passion Flowers, Black Cat Dalia's, Tiger Lilies and just about every single type of beautiful, exotic flower that would not normally be growing together. I was enjoying the moment; the smell of these flowers was absolutely breathtaking. "Hey, June," Amber said as she came and sat down beside me.

I wasn't startled. I knew I was visiting her back yard. I hadn't seen her since I left her behind, so long ago but I certainly always missed her. I reached over and hugged her. "I am really, really, sorry."

She smiled and hugged me back. "For what? You didn't do anything wrong?"

"I left you behind."

"How else was anyone going to tell the story of what happened out there?"

"Story?"

"June, you need to get your life together, and soon. Bad things are coming if you don't wake up."

"Wake up, June, you are spiraling out of control, wake up!"

I startled awake. "Amber?" and saw a guard standing in the door way of my cell.

She looked at me like I was a crazy person. "It's time for your arraignment, let's go."

Dazed and confused, I slid on my fancy jail shoes and followed her out of the cell. I wasn't sure what to make of the experience I had just had. I had not experienced anything like that in a really long time. In fact, not since before I ran away with Amber. It had been so long since I had remembered dreaming that it was nothing but a distant memory – and I didn't miss it at all. I fought the urge to retrace the steps of the dream. I resisted believing that it was real. I eagerly awaited my release from jail so that I could put this dreaming stuff 6 feet underground again.

A detective came to visit and as it would turn out Bob had recently escaped a mental hospital and was considered extremely dangerous. The detective advised, "He has a severe case of schizophrenia, and you're lucky to be alive." The detective made me a deal that if I show him where all of the car keys were, they'd reduce my charges to Receiving Stolen Property which is a lot less severe than Grand Theft Auto. I took the deal. I tried to get Matt the same but since Matt was on parole, he didn't get so lucky. Poor Matt went to prison for being in that truck. I saw him in his holding cell on my way out of jail, I tried to apologize but he wouldn't talk to me.

After I got out of jail I went to Ryan. He said the investigators had been out to see him too and took him for a little ride to get his version of everything that happened. Sadly enough, he couldn't hang out with me anymore so I had to get my stuff and go. The Toyota Bob gave me was also stolen and they had already towed that away.

I was back to square one of homelessness but I didn't dare go back to the Post Office. I began seeking couches and floors that I could sleep on but it seemed like nobody cared about helping unless they were getting something in return. Then I decided that if I just made it a point to stay high all the time the sleeping wouldn't be an issue.

I went to the dealer's house and pitched him a proposal that I run drugs for him. While I was there I met "him." The be all end all of boyfriends, that one boyfriend we have in our lives that we will never, ever, forget.

Twelve

Scratching At The Surface

⁂

Scratching At The Surface

S*cratching At The Surface*
The gates of hell lie just below the surface.
Scratching at the skin, clawing their way out
But never breaking through.
Pulling everything into the vortex of black,
The walls of the vortex
Walls of the prison
That live inside the mind of an addict.
Pulling...
Pulling...
Until the sharp pin prick sets it free.
Nobody ever says, "I want to be a junkie when I grow up," it just happens when the gates of hell need to be opened....

I met a man named Eric who seemed to have it all together. I was extremely interested in him. My dealer was letting me live in the guest house in exchange for housecleaning and babysitting services and Eric was just an added bonus. The number one thing Eric and I didn't have in common was IV drug use. He pitched the experience to me, "Don't knock it till you try it," but I respectfully declined.

Backing up for a second, he didn't just randomly pitch it to me. It came about as a result of my complaining. It was simple, due to the life I had been living, I just didn't get high off of a line of methamphetamine anymore. I still used every single day but my tolerance was just extraordinarily high. In the process of developing this super high tolerance I had also managed to completely destroy my nose. The insides of my nostrils were covered in thick scabs and the exterior of my nose was numb to the touch.

I complained all the time about how damn tired I was, even after snorting lines. Eric said it was time to switch and use it a different way but my dealer, who was kind of a meth mentor advised me to, "Just do more," and laid out a line that was so fricking big I couldn't even snort it all in one take. It took three. Again, I felt nothing.

He and I were always going on about how we were better than the rest of them because we didn't use needles. He'd always tell me, "June, just don't ever fuck up and put a needle in your arm. Lines are harmless, needles are a whole other kind of bad."

Backing up a little more, I had been working with this guy for quite some time. He and I dealt with junkies all day but we were above them and we made that very clear. Depending on what kind of mood I was in I might do something really rude to demonstrate my superiority, like turning down a junkie who was hoping to make a trade for meth, but dumping a large amount of meth onto a carpet right in front of him, rubbing it in with my foot, then sitting back and watching as he picked through all of the carpet fibers. He was desperate for a high and I was looking to drive him crazy so that I could feel superior.

Backing up a little more, again. I was not an inherently mean person. In fact, I was clearly the opposite of mean. Countless times I had sacrificed myself for the sake of another and where did that get me? It never got me anywhere good. I had grown callous and then the meth made me a very uncaring, unfeeling person. When it came to junkies, I was just disgusted at how they behaved.

I had witnessed junkies spending hours locked away in a bathroom, then coming out with these horrible gaping holes in their body. We are talking the size of saucers, having picked at their own flesh, with tweezers, for hours and hours. It was nothing short of a horror movie, but in real life - entire chunks of meat – gone. It sounds crazy and unreal but meth numbs more than just emotional pain – apparently. What it really was is that mind over matter is a powerful thing and to a junkie that's wired. The obsession of digging into their own skin overpowers the pain associated with it.

It made me so sick to see that and I could never understand why junkies were doing that. One day I asked one what that was about, he shoved his arm into my face and pointed at the skin. "Do you see it?"

I looked, I even turned on a light and looked harder. "I see an arm."

"Look! Right there! It's crawling! Right there!"

"What is crawling?"

"THE BUG!" He quietly slumped into a corner and stared at his arm, picking the bugs out for hours upon hours.

This is what I knew of junkies. They were truly the poster children of how a harmless little drug called methamphetamine could absolutely destroy a person. My dealer was my father's age and like a father figure to me. He told me as long as I never stick that needle into my arm I could always have control over the drug and I would never end up like, "those guys." So, I went out of my way to maintain control, even at the expense of the junkies around me. Finding out these guys actually saw bugs crawling under their skin, gave me little more understanding, so I wasn't quite as mean to them anymore. I mean, they were clearly crazy people and in serious need of help. Since I had the meth I helped them, as much as I could.

Eric used needles but he wasn't a "junkie." He was stable and had his life together. I really saw a flawless person in him – especially in comparison to where I had been. So, I had previously classified all needle users as junkies and was now able to see that some still maintain control – they had just opted to use the needle for administration. See how I managed to justify my switch to the needle?

It's amazing how a person can rationalize, justify, and talk themselves into seeing a really dark, dangerous, life-threatening enclosure as a perfectly safe place to be. It's not unlike the way a victim of kidnapping can gradually convince themselves that they have a good life as a prisoner of some psychopath. I describe needles as a hostage situation because that is exactly what it is. Although I had fully rationalized it in my mind, there was a huge part of me, at the very core of my being, that knew exactly what kind of a mess I was stepping into.

Each step I took further into the meth world, was another shred of my self-worth stripping away. What I was really doing was punishing myself. I hated being, me. I hated everything I had done. I was a failure in life who knew I would never amount to anything. I really didn't even try to amount to anything because I simply feared more failure. This gnawed at me from the inside on a daily basis and with each bite into my soul I would sink a little deeper into self-hate and self-abuse. Eric explained that the first shot of meth was a very euphoric experience that made life feel better. That sounded like the words spoken to me the day I tried my first line of meth, I was all in for anything that made me feel better. "Let's do it."

There was one really huge problem with the plan, I was deathly afraid of needles. I mean, I had an insane phobia. I was a person who would actually get dizzy and nauseous at the sight of a needle. He offered to do it for me on one condition. "You can't tell anyone about this."

"Ok."

"Don't even tell them you tried it."

"Ok."

"This stays between me and you."

"Ok, ok, let's just get this done!"

He tried to show me how to prepare a shot but I got all dizzy and couldn't watch so I turned my head and closed my eyes.

"Alright, get ready," he said to me as he tied a tourniquet around my arm. "Little poke."

As I felt the needle penetrate my skin I became very ill, from the thought of what was going on. I could feel vomit rise up to the back of my throat and I got too dizzy to sit up. "Oh God, I'm gonna be sick, I have to lay down." Without allowing myself to look over, I felt the needle pull out of my arm, then I laid on my back, and took a deep breath. "Ok, get it done quick!"

I felt the needle break the skin again, I kept my eyes closed, trying to focus on a grassy meadow.

"Ok, tell me if it hurts."

"Not really."

"There's no burning?"

"No."

"Ok, I'm putting the rest in."

Suddenly, my nausea and dizziness was replaced by a whole-body rush that hit my heart like a freight train. It wasn't a painful freight train, it was a luxury liner that made me cough the moment it hit. Every single molecule of my body felt like it was singing, and I got really turned on. Sex, after my first shot of meth, was also the most euphoric experience of my life.

The next day Eric sat me down and told me, "That feeling you got from the first shot will never happen again. Do not chase it down, the first rush is a one-time experience."

"Why? I want to do it again right now."

"Because of tolerance. If you really want to feel it again you have to increase the dose, but how many times should you increase a dose?"

I didn't care what he was saying to me, I wanted that feeling as many times as I could get it. We left the dealer's house and went to a motel for a while – it was easier to sell product that way. Every time we got high he would step up onto his soap box. "I don't think you should keep using this way."

"Why not, you are?"

"Well, I'm me and you're you. I'm giving you less."

"What the fuck?"

"What are you gonna do about it?" he said as he was giving me my shot.

We checked out of the hotel and everything I owned was in his car - including my clothes. We stopped at a store and I went in to buy cigarettes. When I came out he was gone. He just completely vanished. I wasn't even wearing my shoes. I walked to a friend's house that we were supposed to be going to, assuming he might be there, but he wasn't. They were nice enough to let me hang out and wait for him.

The confines of my mind were like walls slowly closing in. All I could think about was getting high but the sight of a needle still made my head spin. The other thing that made my head spin even faster is that nobody knew I was a junkie except him, which pretty much gave me a way to pretend that I wasn't a junkie. I wrestled with my demons for several days as my life began beating at me from the inside.

Eric became a focus of my rage. I daydreamed of scenarios in which I found him and beat him to death. I felt like out of all of the people in my life who had harmed me, not a single one harmed me as much as he did. It wasn't about the fact that he turned me on to the needle, it was about the fact that he abandoned me without any warning whatsoever. He knew my life depended on him and he left me there to die. That was how severe it was when my "doctor" left me and my access to the needle left with him.

I was ready to die and there was nothing anyone could say to change my mind. I wondered how I would end it all and then decided the most poetic ending to my miserable existence would be an overdose of methamphetamine. The needle was the best way to achieve that but my plans to overdose had to be a secret so I just had one hurdle to face first - the needle.

Coincidentally enough, in my time palling around with my asshole boyfriend we hung out almost exclusively with junkies. So, I didn't have to go anywhere to set my plan into motion, I just came right out and said it. "I've been shooting up for a while now, or, Eric has been doing it for me and I'm jonesing for a shot. I don't know how to do it, can you guys teach me?"

My friends laughed at me. "And she finally comes out of the closet!"

"What?"

Susan walked over. "I was wondering how long you were going to sit there and suffer. I could tell."

I was surprised.

They gave me a crash course in how to shoot up. Susan showed me how to set it up. "So, you take the spoon, and you bend it a little so that it lays flat," she explained as she bent the spoon and gave me a demo of what happens if it doesn't lay flat. "Then you pour the drugs in, how much do you do?"

"I don't know, he always does it for me."

"Well, maybe we should start you with a dime."

"No, give me a quarter."

She laughed and poured about a quarter's worth into the spoon. "Now I'm gonna show you how to tell if you have some good stuff." She grabbed a brand new 50cc needle out of a bag, and used a glass of water that was sitting there to draw up 10cc's of water. She squirted the water into the spoon then flipped the syringe over and used it to smash the rocks of meth. Then she grabbed a cigarette butt and ripped a small piece of cotton from the filter. "Take a small piece of cotton and roll it up into a tight little ball."

She used the tips of her fingers to roll it. "This is VERY important, you don't want to inject cotton fibers, they'll make you really sick." Then she dropped the cotton into the center of the spoon and pressed the tip of the needle into the cotton to draw up the load. She drew up all of the liquid. "Remember how much water we put in?" She held the syringe up to me. "Look it that, 23cc's. That's good stuff." She smiled with pride. "Now for the fun part."

She handed me a tie. "Which vein did he use on you?" I held out my arm and pulled up my long sleeve to expose the huge bruise on my forearm. "Do you want to try and use the same one? It's kind of hard to see."

"I don't know." I was fighting to keep the room from spinning at the sight of the needle, the nausea was almost unbearable.

"Tie this around your arm really tight and pump your fist."

I tied it around my arm and pumped my fist. She helped me look for a vein, once we found one she handed me the needle. "Here, slide it in a 30-degree angle." She grabbed another needle and showed me on herself.

I felt vomit slowly creeping up into my throat as I struggled to keep my vision stable – the dizziness was winning. It was a good thing I was sitting down or I would have already fallen down. I was on a suicide mission, I had to focus, I couldn't be weak about it. I took in a few deep breaths and I stuck the needle into my arm. Sadly enough, just sticking it into my arm wasn't enough, I had to actually find a vein. I rotated it around with her help but had no luck and pulled it out. "Am I doing it wrong?"

"Yes, I don't think the angle is right. Let's look for another one." She helped me search and try for a long, long time. I felt like a human pin cushion. I was so mad. This was supposed to be a statement to the world, my way of telling everyone to fuck off, and I couldn't do it. I just couldn't. In the process of my frustration, my phobia of needles and my death wish moved aside, replaced by the desperation of a junkie trying to get high and replaced by the actual relationship that had made me so depressed.

"Susan, will you hit me?" She hesitated, it wasn't something she wanted to do.

"I don't want to, what if something goes wrong? Let's just keep trying this."

"But I'm so frustrated and my arm hurts. Please!"

"I'll get Paul, he's good at this stuff."

She returned with Paul a few minutes later and he was able to give me the shot. The euphoria was back and I wasn't so ready to off myself anymore. It's amazing how a little bit of drugs can change an entire outlook on life. Sadly, I still couldn't do it myself but I spent countless hours and hours trying. It's a lot like trying to draw something and failing so many times that the eraser just won't clean the page anymore.

There was a lot of blood, a lot of torn skin, a lot of bruises and I liked the pain. It's funny how a healthy dose of external pain can ease the pain of years of torment constantly pushing against the confines of the insides, looking for a way to break out. The punctures in the skin gave that pain an escape – it was the first time in my life that I actually found a little bit of peace. I wanted more than just a little…I wanted it all…as I was bleeding out from the inside. In this moment, I no longer cared about the boyfriend who abandoned me either. As it would turn out, he wasn't the one I was so sad about losing. It was the needle.

Thirteen

Bridges To Nowhere

*T*his is the way the world ends.
Not with a bang, but with a whimper.
(T.S. Elliott)

Slamming dope was a new way of life for me and hunting for the perfect vein was my biggest obsession. I didn't really understand or know who I was anymore. I would slip into a bathroom, lock the door and time would pass as people knocked on the door hoping to use the bathroom. Oftentimes I would spend hours and hours in there. It was more of a vein hunting expedition than it was an opportunity to get high. A lot of times I never even did the shot.

It was my intention to do the shot but I would hit a vein; the blood would flood the syringe and then instead of pushing the syringe's plunger down I would pull it out and poke a new hole for a different vein. Then after obsessing for an unspecified amount of time, the blood would start to actually coagulate and clot up inside of the barrel, plugging up the syringe.

If I had more syringes and more drugs I'd put together a new shot. Most of the time I didn't, so, the process of popping off the needle tip, squirting the bloody drugs back into the spoon, then filtering it through the cotton, and shooting up the bloody meth became pretty common. Sometimes the needle would be completely wrecked and that's when I learned about butt shots.

A butt shot is a strange experience that doesn't give the same rush as shooting up but it gets the drugs into the system so it works in a pinch. It is exactly how it sounds, pop the tip off of the syringe, insert the syringe into the butt and then push the drugs in. It is quickly absorbed into the system. I learned about this method from a junkie friend who used butt shots, exclusively. It was surprisingly popular but I personally couldn't see what all the fuss was about. I preferred the rush associated with the vein although sometimes I wondered what it was I truly loved the most: the sight of the blood or the rush of the drugs. I knew I was sick. I knew this had gone way too far but I needed it. I couldn't live without it. It was an irresistible aching need that helped me feel better, period.

Bridges never burned so quickly than they did when I started hijacking the bathrooms of my friends and acquaintances and eventually nobody wanted me to come to their house. I was out in the world completely alone again, and without any drugs. The confines of my insides began to push against the seams again, in an unbearable way, that's when I decided it was time.

I went to a store and shoplifted as many boxes of sleeping pills I could fit into my pockets which was about 6 or 7 boxes. I then went to a fast food restaurant and got myself a complimentary glass of water. Then I walked over to a church, it was late at night, I sat on the steps. I sat there because even though I was not religious and I had no religious upbringing, I was still angry at God and religion nonetheless.

Being on the front steps of that church was my way of telling God, Christianity, Catholics, the be all end all of religion to go fuck themselves. Although they never did anything to me, per se, I was still pissed at the idea of hope that they were peddling out of these places. I popped all of the sleeping pills out of the little packets and put them into a little pile on the concrete. Then I scooped them all up and shouted, "Every single person on this planet can just fuck off!" And I swallowed them all.

As I sat there I realized I was too visible and feared someone would spot me and try to save me. That someone being Deputy Corbin, since we seemed to have a knack for running into each other at my most inopportune times and I couldn't let that happen, so I walked to the river.

There was a very secluded boat dock I had been to a lot when I wanted privacy. I knew it would be deserted this late at night, so I walked out to the end of the dock, and laid down to contemplate my miserable life while I waited to fall asleep. There was absolutely no chance that anyone would be able intervene so I laid there with full confidence that it would be the last waking moment of my misery.

There was honestly a big part of me that felt no one would even care enough to intervene, and I think I preferred the not knowing. I knew my dad would care but I knew I'd have miles to go before I would ever be seeing him again. I cried a little at the thought of him. I loved him, I really did, but I was incapable of showing that. I was incapable of anything that wasn't self-serving at this point, as I had been swallowed whole by my own self-hatred. I was only 20 years old, but if the rest of my days were going to be anything like the 20 I'd already lived, I'd just have to pass. I felt a twinge of pride about what I was doing, in this moment. It felt like the first time in my life that I was in control. I made a choice and I followed through.

I closed my eyes and started seeing flashes from my childhood. I saw a butterfly. It was the most beautiful thing I had ever seen in my life. It had every single color of the rainbow and an enormous wing span like no other. I ran over to it and discovered that one of its absolutely gorgeous wings was stuck to the pavement. I watched it struggling to break free, but the wing was completely saturated. I had been playing in the sprinkler and this beautiful creature was stuck in the water.

It was my fault.

I suddenly felt a tickle on my nose, and I awoke in a park, it was really dark, but I watched the butterfly crawl around my face for a second and then fly away. I got up and followed it, taken up in the chase I momentarily forgot where I was and what I was doing. I was a little confused about the butterfly, seeing as it was really dark outside, I was trying to remember if I had ever seen a butterfly at night. "Hey June, what's going on?" I spun around, startled by the male voice and saw Lucas walking beside me. I hadn't seen him in a really, really, long time. The reality of what I was doing out there suddenly crashed in on me and I felt even more confused. A part of me longed to go back to the boat dock I was laying on but I just kept walking.

I reached down into my purse to pull out a cigarette, and lit one. "I haven't seen you in years, what are you doing here?"

"Oh, just walking to a friends."

As he was talking, I was zoning out. The cigarette I was smoking had disappeared. I went to take a drag from it and my hand was empty. I stopped, looked around on the ground for it but it wasn't there. I lit another one and kept walking as he was talking to me. I only heard his voice droning on in an inaudible way as yet another cigarette vanished from my hand, into thin air.

"Hey, can I get a cigarette?"

I kept lighting them and dropping them but I didn't know where they were going.

"Good luck, man."

I lit another one myself but the same damn thing kept happening. I watched him and he seemed to be doing fine. What kind of hell did I wake up in?

"What are you doing out here, June?"

"Oh, just waiting to die."

He laughed. "Aren't we all?"

I stopped walking. "I'm actually gonna go lay down in the park for a while."

He reached out and gently grabbed my arm. "Come on and walk with me. I haven't seen you in years, I'd love to talk some more." Something about his touch was undeniable, it was almost magnetic. I felt compelled to listen, so I stuck with him. We walked and talked for what felt like hours, then eventually made our way over to a waist high cement wall that we both sat down on. He told me all about his life and where he lived.

I remember thinking to myself that I was never sure where I knew this guy from or how it is that we had known each other for so long, but we had somehow known each other for years. I told him about the life I had fallen into and how miserable I was. I told him about LA and he was surprised but assured me, "LA is no place for a girl with nowhere to go – it's good that you didn't. But, you can totally do anything with your life that you want to do. I want you to remember there are people in this world who care about you. This life you're so miserable about can always be changed, you have the power to change it. But if you off yourself, this life that you hate so much, this person you say that you have become, is all you will ever have a chance to be."

"It's too late, man, I took a lot of pills tonight, enough to finish me off."

"Well, with all the walking you just did there may be hope for you yet." He winked, smiled, and walked away.

I was pretty out of it and doubly confused about what just happened, I made another attempt to smoke though, but this time when I reached down I discovered I didn't even have any cigarettes or a purse. My reality had somehow shifted as I realized I never had a purse or cigarettes on me to begin with. Once again, I was really out of it and confused.

Then suddenly, out of seemingly nowhere, that damn Deputy Corbin walked up. I suspected I was seeing things, I rubbed my eyes and looked again. Sure as shit, there he was, all judgmental and smiling at me. "What's wrong, June, you look like you just seen a ghost or something?" Then I saw his car as two more cop cars pulled up. "What kinda drugs you been using tonight?" He shined a flashlight in my face, I shielded my eyes from the light.

I was so pissed, I was certain that old friend of mine had slipped away and called the police on me. I wasn't going to admit to ANYTHING. So tired of people being all nosy, acting like they cared when nobody understood, nobody understood anything, my life was a steaming pile of dog shit. "Shitty, you?"

A fire truck pulled up.

"What did you take, June?"

"Nothing, why do you just walk up assuming I took something?"

Then an ambulance pulled up.

"What the hell are they doing here?"

"We got a call, we just wanna make sure you're ok."

A medic walked up.

"Let him take a look at you, June."

The medic reached out for my wrist and felt my pulse. "What did you take, ma'am?" he asked while Corbin shined the flashlight in my face again. I stood there and let them give me the once over while adamantly denying that I took anything at all.

"Nothing."

"Then why are you swaying like this?" He pointed at my legs.

"Tired."

"Do you feel like you need help? We can take you to the hospital right now."

"No, I don't need any help."

The medic turned to Sheriff Corbin. "We can take her in and pump her stomach but she has to agree to treatment, we can't force her to go."

"June, I want you to get into the ambulance." Corbin grabbed my arm/ "Let them help you."

I pulled away. "No."

"At least tell us what you took."

"I said I didn't take anything."

"Well then why did I get calls about you wandering down alleyways, talking to people who weren't there and looking in people's windows?"

"I didn't do any of that, and I was talking to a friend."

"How many people do you see here right now?"

A second deputy stepped in and started shining a light in my eyes again. "No one! All I see is light!" He stepped back and turned the light away from my face.

"I see three, there's three cops and those guys in the ambulance."

Corbin nodded to the deputy. "Give her a field test." Corbin stepped away and radioed to dispatch while the Deputy put me through the paces of a field sobriety test. A little while later some guys pulled up in an unmarked car. "June, these guys are specialists. If you took something, they're gonna know. Why don't you save us all the time and trouble? Tell us what you took."

I shook my head.

The "specialists" put me through a bunch of tests too and then shook their

92

heads at Corbin. "Do you have a place to stay?"

I shook my head in shame.

"Well, I can't just let you wander the streets this way. Set her down in the back of my car."

The deputy stepped up and guided me to the back seat of the patrol car then walked over to reconvene with Corbin. I started considering fessing up. I did not want to go to jail, I really had not even done anything wrong. If I wanted to die it was my business and I wasn't about to cry on Corbin's shoulder about it. But, on second thought. "Hey!" I shouted to the Deputy, "get Corbin!"

Corbin walked over to the car to talk to me. "I think I have a place to go, but I'm not sure."

"As long as it ain't the post office we can give it a try," he joked with me, but wasn't really laughing.

I gave him directions to one of my friend's houses. "I don't know for sure if they'll let me stay, they kind of kicked me out already."

"I'll talk to them and see what they say. If they don't, I'm taking you to mental health. I can't let you wander the streets in your condition."

"I don't need to go to mental health."

"June, I know you took something, I know you. I wish that you would just let us help you." I stared out the window quietly while he spoke to me. "You're so young, you have so much potential in life, it pains me to do this job and see people like you wasting away out here. It's filthy disgusting, sometimes I just want to." He stopped talking. "I can't shake the feeling that I'm making a mistake right now. I think I should take you to mental health, my patience is wearing thin with you. I think one of these days I'll be finding your body out here somewhere, in pieces."

I rolled my eyes, totally over the idea that anyone gave a shit. "Wonder how many pieces I'll be in?"

I agitated him, it was clear. "Now see, you start saying shit like that and I'll have half a mind to-"

"I'm sorry, I'm just tired. Thank you for giving me a ride and helping."

Sheriff Corbin seemed like he cared but I was struggling to figure him out, he was definitely a little rougher around the edges than he was the last time I talked to him. Being a cop must be hard, because I know being a homeless junkie was absolutely fucking impossible. I just hoped that my friends let me stay, then I could proceed with my plans that had been rudely interrupted by this do-gooder.

Corbin pulled into the apartment complex. "I'm not letting you out till I know you have somewhere to go, let me talk to them first." He parked and went to the door. He was there talking to them for a while. It was late, I figured they weren't too happy about being woken up, or that the knock on the door was about me. The riff-raff they already threw out once before when my drug habit got exposed. Technically, I only had one friend here. We'd known each other for years, but this was her boyfriend's place. He was a Marine, and he threw me out on my ass faster than the blink of an eye. Corbin returned to the car and opened my door. "Come on, he's gonna let you spend the night here." I climbed out of the car anxious to know what was said at the front door.

"Really? What'd he say?"

Corbin ignored my question as he began his lecture. "Listen, June, it's time to grow the fuck up. No one can help someone who won't help themselves and soon, there'll be no one left in this world willing to help you. The next time I see you I can promise you I won't be so nice. I am done. You've used up all your favors here, understand?"

I nodded my head.

"This is a small town and I know everybody in it. I have tried to be nice but you won't listen. From now on when we see you on the street, we'll make it a point to check on you but if you're still up to no good, you'll find your life can get pretty miserable."

I nodded my head as I tried to process what he was saying, I was still really out of it though. "Get inside, don't let me catch you out on the street or I'll throw your ass in mental health and make sure you stay for a long, long, while. Got it?"

"Yes," I replied as I awkwardly walked towards the door, it was wide open but there was nobody there to greet me. I went to the hideaway bed that I slept on when I stayed there before and laid down.

I pondered how screwed up it was to have Corbin bring me here. They had already thrown me out over my drug use. Then on the night I decided to end it all, I return there and get back inside through the help of the cops. The irony is, they made me leave so I wouldn't bring ugliness into their house. Yet I laid down in their living room with the hopes that I would never wake up again. It was a truly selfish act and I knew they'd be really pissed but I didn't care. I passed out quickly.

There's an inner voice that everyone possesses.

It holds the power to do wondrous things.

This is the voice within that tells us "you can do it!"

But, for some people it can be a more ominous voice, a constant reminder of failure.

We are the creators of that voice, and we hold the power to change it.

Life is a series of consequences,

each action paying in kind.

And each day a new beginning –

Each day offers a chance to do it all over again.

That's both the beauty and the greatest gift

in this hellhole world.

Each day is a chance to right the wrongs of yesterday,

Or the chance to live with the consequences of yesterday.

What about when each day is a living reminder of 15 years of yesterday's?

What happens when 15 years of yesterday's look exactly like 15 years of tomorrow?

I think that's the point where a person just gives up.

It's the inner voice reminding us that all of our tomorrows will be exactly same as the rotting sack of shit our yesterday was.

That kind of life just isn't worth living, it is a life of captivity in a self-built prison.

I woke up. I looked around the room and locked eyes with a disgruntled Marine who was throwing grapes at my face. "Finally, five fucking days later."

I sat up, trying to register where I was and what had happened. "What?"

"You've been asleep for five days. What in the hell did you take?"

My head was spinning too fast to stay upright, I collapsed back down. "Sleeping pills."

"Wait a second, you had the cops ask me to let you spend the night, after taking a bunch of sleeping pills? Seriously?" He stood up and dropped the bowl of grapes next to my head. "Eat, use the bathroom, do what you need, you got 30 minutes to get out of my house, do not ever come back." He walked out of the room.

"Ok."

He walked back into the room. "And I don't care if the cops are knocking, I don't care if there's a zombie apocalypse outside, I don't care if you're bleeding to death, NO MORE!"

I got up, steadied myself, used the bathroom, and left. I had no interest in sticking around somewhere that I wasn't wanted, which is exactly why I took those sleeping pills. It was amazing, I really put both feet forward with those sleeping pills. I even resisted confessing to the police about it, I went out of my way and look at where I was. I knew in that moment that God was real, and that He absolutely hated me. Any God that would force me to continue in my life, in my world, was a hateful one indeed. I also learned that there was no way out of this shithole and whoever said dying was the easy way out was a bold-faced liar because that shit was hard.

Fourteen

The Abyss

I walked down the street into the Abyss of hell. That's how I viewed my world. It was bloody, bruised, wrecked, it smelled, and I wanted to go home but had no home to go to. I was so sick of people telling me there was hope. I was so sick of people telling me to get my shit together. My big burning question was simple HOW?! How in the hell was I supposed to ever do anything different? I had nowhere to live, I had nothing but the methamphetamine and needles. The only friends I had to speak of were junkies.

I had contemplated offing myself for years but the sleeping pill experiment was the truest attempt ever. I swear I did everything right and it made no sense that I survived. One might think I'd wake up refreshed and maybe be happy I survived. But hey, I woke up to the same scowling I had grown accustomed to. I sometimes wondered if people knew I was a living, breathing person.

Did people know that I was an actual person who needed shelter, food and somewhere to belong, just like everyone else? I mean shit, when I was 13 I was nothing but a sexual object to everyone. As a junkie, nothing but a junkie and sex object to everyone. I was really sick and tired of the world of scowling, judgement and everyone telling me I needed to do better.

I needed to go hang out with some non-judgmental people, so I decided to go visit my friends Mike and Sue. They had finally moved out of the motel and into a house. I hadn't seen them in a long, long time. Michael had grown a lot but was as quiet as ever. I sat and colored with him. "How you been, buddy?" He smiled back at me but didn't respond. I thought there was something kind of "off" about him. He seemed really pale. "You wanna go outside and play?"

Sue shouted from the bedroom. "He's not allowed outside, he's grounded cause he's a little brat!"

"Oh, ok."

Sue came out into the living room. "That bitch neighbor across the street called Child Services on us for not letting him play outside." She sat on the couch next to me, lit a cigarette and blew the smoke in Michael's face. "I told her to fuck off and that if she didn't shut her mouth I'd shut if for her, then she pressed charges against me for verbal assault." Sue got up and stomped into the kitchen.

"Are you fucking kidding me? I didn't even know that was a thing. Did they arrest you?"

She shouted to me from the kitchen, "It's a fucking ticket, I gotta go to court." She came back with a beer and plopped down on the couch next to me. "So, I'm not letting him go out there cause God knows what she's gonna say, he's fine in here." She turned on the TV to a cartoon and went back into her room. The situation there was awkward but I stayed for a couple of days and watched over Michael. He seemed ok but his mother acted like she just did not like him and I wasn't sure why. Mike and I chatted about cooking our own meth and all the money we could make but Sue was suddenly the sane one and threw a big fit so that was out.

I took off after a couple of days so as to not overstay my welcome. I couldn't speak on how she was treating her kid either because again – overstay my welcome. One thing I knew for sure is that she wasn't hitting him, she just wasn't uplifting him. A deep part of me knew that it was another form of abuse, and I wished him better. It definitely wasn't garnering a lot of self-confidence for the kid but luckily, he was the apple of his father's eye and he was in good hands – or so it seemed.

Once I was out and about again I met the next boyfriend Justin who fortunately had his own place. Jackpot. Unfortunately, he had just been evicted and would be out on the streets in a couple of weeks. We actually already knew each other from before I became a junkie and he was very excited to find out that I had joined him. It makes things easier when two people are into the same things. When it comes to sex he asked me what my favorites were. I shrugged. He asked me point blank, "What gives you an orgasm?" Sadly, I didn't know what that was. Then he said, "Well, it's time to find out."

I have to say that having an orgasm was the most interesting experience ever. The rush of heat that filled my body was better than a shot of meth. I could not believe that out of all of the years I had been sexually active I had never once experienced an orgasm. He became my new favorite person, so when he asked me to marry him two weeks later, I dove right in.

We planned to have the wedding at the beach, then for our honeymoon we wanted to do something crazy – rafting down the river rapids in the middle of the night. We had a tiny little bit of money from government assistance and drug dealing so we got a motel room at one of those scummy places where people live full time. It was the perfect location for our business and business was booming.

On the night of our wedding we planned on heading to the river but getting away from the room proved to be a challenge. I was locked away in the bathroom but I was having the time of my junkie life because it was my very own bathroom, so I could stay in there for as long as I wanted to.

I was startled by a knock on my bathroom window, it was my friend Mike, he slid the window open and poked his head in. "What's shakin?"

"We're going river rafting. Wanna come?"

"I'll pass." Mike looked down at my arm. "You got more?"

"I got lots." I reached into my pocket and tossed him a baggie.

"Nice!" He took it and left.

I resumed my vein hunting obsession. This was what I did. Tweakers all have a thing that they like to tweak on when they're wired. Some of the sicker ones like to hunt and catch bugs crawling under their skin. Some like to dig through trash cans. I knew some who liked to pilfer through the contents of vacuums at car washes.

In my early years of using meth I enjoyed going crystal hunting. That's when we would spend hours in areas known for lots of quartz crystals. We'd find the quartz rocks, crack them open, and get beautiful crystal stones to make jewelry. I once stayed out there in the heat for so long that I couldn't speak for days, having lost my voice from the dehydration. These days, my tweek was looking for veins. It was my favorite thing to do when I was wired, but I not only looked, I poked. Then even if I hit a vein I'd still look for another one. I always enjoyed finding a vein with the fastest blood flow, then the winning spot would be rewarded as my primary vein for as long as it survived my abuse, before vanishing from the surface.

This was my thing and it was well known throughout the meth world of my friends, so having my own bathroom was a time when I could proudly stay in there for as long as I wanted, without the interruptions of judgmental people trying to use the toilet. People were so rude sometimes, why couldn't they just pee outside? Then, it happened, I found the winning vein. "Hey!" Then I shoved the needle right through it, startled by Mike.

"Dude!" I pulled the needle out as he laughed at me.

"How fucking long you gonna poke yourself?"

"Hey, this is my bathroom." I smiled at him.

"You guys interested in trading for some acid? I got a guy out here."

"I don't know." I stepped out of the bathroom to talk to Justin. "Do we want acid?"

"Yes!" Justin hustled into the bathroom to chat with Mike through the window.

"Alright, I'll be right back." Mike disappeared.

Justin went back to whatever he was doing, I went back to my sickness, and eventually Mike returned. While he was there doing the deal, he gave me the 411 on what to expect when we headed out to the river. "OK, June, there's SWAT all throughout the woods between the motel and the river."

"Ahh shit! Why?"

"I don't know what's going on but I'll keep you posted."

"Great, thanks man."

"Over and out," he said as he stepped away from the window.

I went back to what I was doing in the bathroom, same ol' same ol', poking holes in the arm. A while later he knocked on the window again. "Alright, there's more of them now but I think they're watching the motel next door. Also, I got a guy who needs a quarter." He showed me $20.

I set my needle down and grabbed him a quarter.

"Alright, I'll let you know what's happening with the SWAT."

"Alright, thanks for looking out for us, man."

"Hey, anytime, you know you're like a sister to me."

"I love you, man."

"Peace out."

He walked off and I shut the window again.

I finally stepped out of the bathroom to talk to my husband. "I just sold a quarter to Mike." I tossed the money on the bed.

He nodded at the bathroom. "You're more talented than I thought."

"Mike says there's SWAT all over the place out there." Justin didn't seem to care. I went back into the bathroom as Mike returned.

"If you guys go to the river, make sure you stay low and keep to the bushes," he said, and then took off again.

Justin stepped into the bathroom. "Let's do this!" He handed me a half a hit, and offered one to Mike who declined. I put it on my tongue, Justin put two whole hits in his own mouth.

Mike laughed. "You guys are fucking crazy!" He poked his head in through the window. "You do know there's SWAT all over the place?"

Justin laughed at him. "They don't give a shit about a couple of people going to the river."

"Oh yeah, rafting in the middle of the night is totally normal," Mike said as he reached in to grab a cigarette off the back of the toilet. "I'm out, good luck." Then he disappeared.

Justin grabbed the raft. "Let's go on our honeymoon." Then hand and hand we walked out of the room.

I was tripping. "What about the SWAT team?"

"They don't care about us," he said as he dragged me along.

The woods that led to the river were literally right behind the motel, I spotted men in black SWAT gear and I ran for the cover of the trees. I was ducking, dodging, diving into bushes and low crawling my way through while he was calmly walking. He laughed at me. "Get up and walk."

I poked my head out of a bush in a shouting kind of a whisper, "No!"

We finally reached the clearing to the river when a spotlight lit us up. I screamed, "Tuck and roll!" and dove down an embankment, rolling to the river's edge.

Justin just stood there, I couldn't believe my eyes.

"What the fuck are you doing? You're gonna get us caught!"

He pointed across the river. "That was a car over there, turning around." Then he pulled the raft out of the box and started airing it up with a little hand pump. I was keeping point, watching every single bush, then I saw a Sheriff's patrol car pull up and I started trying to hide under the deflated raft. It wasn't working so I rolled onto my back and was attempting to dig myself deeper into the dirt so I would camouflage myself but that shit wasn't working either. Justin was getting agitated with me as he was struggling to pump up the raft. "Knock it off! There ain't nothing there!"

"You have to hurry up! That raft is our only escape!" I shoved him down and took over the pump, erratically pumping it. Justin got back up and tried to get it back but I broke it and immediately blamed him. "Now look what you did, asshole!"

Justin ignored me and started airing it up with his mouth.

I got up, pacing anxiously and rambling to myself. "What the fuck am I gonna do now?"

Justin chimed in, "It's almost ready."

I could hear him but I wasn't rational, I took off into the river to swim. It didn't take me long to jump right back out due to the freezing cold temperatures then, just when my insanity was reaching the breaking point Justin stood up with the inflated raft. "See!"

"Oh, thank God, hurry the fuck up!"

I snatched it from him and threw it into the river, eager to get away from all of the men hiding in the bushes. We paddled out into the rapids under the light of the full moon. Once we were far away from the shore, we relaxed and coasted for a while. I was burning up so I started hanging over the side, drinking the water and splashing it on my face.

"You shouldn't drink that," Justin said.

"I'm so hot I can hardly breathe." I kept splashing myself with the cold river water.

"Well that's probably because of the acid and the running."

Then I saw the most terrifying thing ever. It looked like some kind of a sea monster was slowly approaching the raft. It was huge. I stared at it, trying to focus in on what I was seeing with nothing but the aid of the moonlight. Then, it finally came into focus. It was a monster sized duck. Not just one, there was a whole gang of them circling our raft like a bunch of sharks. I screamed and moved to the other side of the raft, trying to distance myself but they were surrounding us! Then they came in closer and they were pecking at the raft. We were under attack. I grabbed an oar and swung it but they were spry and kept ducking out of the way! Justin tried to grab the oar and we wrestled with it back and forth nearly tipping the raft. "They're gonna pop the raft and eat us!" I wrestled it away from him and kept trying to protect us. "Just trying to save your life!"

He caught me off guard and took the oar away. Then turned me around, looked me in the eyes and said, "Have you ever used acid before?"

"Maybe once, years ago."

"Ok, well, those are just Canadian geese, and they are just looking to see if we have any food." He smiled at me. "You're having a bad trip." Then he paddled and got us a short distance from the enemy. "See? They aren't even chasing us." I had a break in the insanity for a brief moment and realized I was having one of those red and green spider moments.

I looked deep into his eyes, the eyes of the man I'd just married, the eyes of the man I was on my honeymoon with, as the moon shined on his face in a very special way and that was when I saw it. That was the moment that I suddenly knew. He was a complete stranger. I suddenly knew I had married a complete stranger for the sake of being able to pretend I had someone in my life who cared about me. It was for the sake of having a place to live. I had basically sold myself to this - monster. The moment the reality of this hit, I saw him, under the light of the moon and he had this ugliness about him that I had never even noticed before.

I wanted as far away from him as I could possibly get. It was a strange moment of sanity, at an insane time, because I suddenly knew I was only with him because I was so lost in life that I needed an escape, a reprieve, from the apathy, loneliness and despair. At that moment the old me, the one I had forgotten in the short time I'd been seeing him, came crashing in, and there I was again. Wondering how long I would stick around until I was sleeping on the floor of the Post Office again. I sat back in the raft and tried to relax, always keeping an eye on the monstrous killer ducks. While the misery of my life crashed in. The bad trip was over, and it was no match for my reality.

A little while later we paddled over to the private dock at someone's house. We had no idea whose house it was but my limbs were literally frozen from all of the time I had spent dangling in the freezing cold river. Justin and I hung from the dock catching white water from the surface and drinking it. River water is supposedly really nasty but that was the best damn ice water I had ever had.

The sun began to rise, the warmth was refreshing, I laid on the dock in the sun and the only word I could mutter out of my mouth was "melting." We eventually got up and walked through the person's backyard, found a pay phone, called a taxi and went back to the hotel. When Justin reached for me in bed I rolled away and made excuses. I didn't ever want him to touch me again. I was done.

We got kicked out of the motel room and started sleeping in his old beat up car. We kept it parked at the motel and nobody cared that we lived there in it. The dislike I had developed for him on the river rafting excursion had done nothing but grow and grow, constantly intensified by the way he would disappear. It's not that he had no right to go off and do stuff alone. It was the way he would say he'd be right back and then that would turn into an entire week of wondering where in the hell he was.

One day he was gone and I needed a private place to do a shot. I asked Stacey, a nice, single mom if I could use her bathroom she said, "As long as you're not using, cause I'm trying to stay clean. I got 14 days."

"Oh no, I just need to pee and take a shower."

"Ok," she said as she let me in.

She really shouldn't have done that, she should have trusted her instincts. I felt kinda bad but not bad enough to stop. I made up my mind that I wanted to try shooting up in my neck, and I needed a mirror to do it. Once I got the shot ready I started rooting around the side of my neck for a vein. I had no idea how to shoot up in my neck, I had just heard that it's a better rush so I assumed that any vein would do. There's these veins in the side of the neck that sit literally right below the ears. There's also a lot of cartilage there.

I got lucky and hit a vein right away. I wanted to be sure so I double checked by pulling the plunger back one more time, but there wasn't any more blood. Injecting meth outside of a vein inevitably leads to an abscess and the neck is the last place a person wants one of those. I dug around in my neck a little bit, then when my arms got tired I pulled out, and tugged, and tugged, and tugged but the needle wouldn't budge.

I could actually see it, on the inside of my skin, pressing against the skin from the inside. It was like the needle had somehow bent into a capital L shape instead of a straight needle. I kept rotating it, trying to wiggle it out of my neck but it would not come out. Stacey knocked on the door. "Are you gonna get into the shower soon? Cause I put my son to bed in a half hour and I don't want you to wake him up."

I yelled to her, "Yeah, in a minute, still on the toilet."

I had no idea what to do, I kept pulling and getting nowhere. My neck was starting to swell up. I turned on the shower so Stacey would think I was in there. Then I opened the bathroom window and luckily, I spotted my friend Mike skulking around. I got his attention with a loud whisper, hoping Stacy couldn't hear me over the shower. "Hey!" I waved him over. "I need help."

He walked over a few feet from the window. "What's up?"

"Promise you won't laugh."

He got this shit eating grin on his face and walked in really close. "What's going on?"

I turned and showed him the needle, it was hanging out of my neck, but sticking out horizontally. He busted up laughing. "How in the fuck did you do that?"

"Shhhhh, I'm not supposed to be doing this in here."

He covered his mouth, face bright red from the laughter.

"What do I do?"

"How the fuck should I know?"

"You have to help me!"

"What in the hell happened?"

"I don't know!"

"Maybe you can go to the hospital?"

"Wait, you're saying just walk down the street with a needle hanging out of my fucking neck?"

"Wrap it in a towel or something." He laughed at me and walked away, then pointed a finger over his shoulder in my direction adding, "and that, is why I don't shoot up." I flipped him off and closed the window.

I tried and tried to pull it but it wouldn't budge. I imagined walking down the street to the ER with a towel draped around my neck as Deputy Corbin spotted me and decided to see exactly what was going on. I wondered what I would say, or even better, I wondered what he would say. I imagined this, right here, was about to be the most embarrassing moment of my life. My waking nightmare was halted by more pounding on the bathroom door, I shouted kind of irritably, "I, am, almost, DONE!"

I turned off the shower and prepared myself mentally for walking out of the bathroom, needle and all. I looked at myself in the mirror, took a deep breath, my shoulders fell in a moment of surrendering to my fate and VOILA! The needle fell out. What a relief! I put it in my pocket and rushed out of the bathroom. "Thank you!" I said to Stacey as I scurried past her and right out of that room.

As soon as I got outside I spotted Justin tweaking in the car. I rushed over and hopped in. "We need to get the fuck out of here, right now, and find a place to live that isn't in a goddamned car. NOW!" He stopped what he was doing, started the car and drove. I was running from myself, but every ounce of me was angry at the car. Angry at the motel. Angry at the nice woman who let me use her bathroom. More importantly, I was angry at that fucking Justin. It was everyone else's fault, as I looked at my neck in the mirror, rubbing the lump and wondering if my neck was going to be alright.

"Where do you want to go?"

"I don't fucking know! Let's go to that lady Tabitha's house."

On the way, the car started acting up, and was barely running as we pulled into Tabitha's driveway, "Maybe we can hang out here while I get it fixed?"

"Yeah, we'll see." I got out, rushed to the front door and pounded.

Tabitha opened the door and gave me a big welcoming smile. I pulled out my bent syringe. "You got a point?"

Tabitha looked at my L shaped needle. "Damn, girl, what the fuck did you do? Come on in."

She let us in and I told the horrible story of, um, the strangely shaped needle. She looked at my neck, Justin tried to look but I batted him away. She gave me one of her old needles and some bleach to clean it. I went into the bathroom and used a vein in my arm to get some drugs in quickly. I guess the whole neck experience had temporarily halted my obsession to spend countless hours screwing around with it.

Later into the night, Justin pulled me aside to talk. "I spotted a car a few blocks away that I could use for parts to fix ours."

"Please, don't go anywhere. Every time you go somewhere I sit around looking like a dumbass, waiting for you to come back."

"I won't be gone long."

"Yes, you fucking will!"

"It's just down the street."

"Listen to me, asshole, you embarrass me in front of Tabitha and I'll be so done with you it'll make your head spin. Got it?"

He dropped his head, almost as if in shame. "Fine. I won't go anywhere. But we're gonna be stuck on foot till this gets fixed."

"We will find another way, do not steal that damn car!" I shouted at him and walked into the bathroom. I was feeling like my old self again so I stepped into the bathroom and proceeded to vacate my reality. When I finally emerged from the bathroom, Justin was gone.

Tabitha poked her head out of her bedroom. "He said to tell you he walked to the store."

I felt a big knot in my stomach that quickly turned to rage. "Oh my fucking God, he's gonna be gone for days, what the fuck am I gonna do?"

"What do you mean? He said he was gonna get you a soda and some smokes?"

I walked into Tabitha's room and gave her whole low down of what he always does. She smiled at me. "Just hang out here, it's cool."

As I predicted, Justin never came back. A few days later we spotted the article in the newspaper. He'd been caught stealing a car. The situation was a pretty big deal that landed on the front page of the newspaper. The only reason he got caught was because the car he stole was out of gas. He managed to get it to the gas station but the gas cap had a lock on it. It seemed suspicious when a man was seen breaking into the gas cap of a car, at the gas pumps.

Long story short, he was going away for a long while. I have to confess, I found it a little humorous. I had warned him, I knew it was not going to end well, but he went off and did it anyways. Tabitha and I were fast friends, but I felt like an abandoned cat on her doorstep, which was a little bit awkward. She told me I was the coolest abandoned cat she ever had the pleasure of taking in. I was happy that she felt that way and a part of me was grateful to have somewhere but it was overshadowed by a dark apathy that was impossible to shake.

There was a cemetery a few blocks away from her house. I found myself walking over there, sitting on graves, and feeling really jealous that they were dead. I was jealous they had already walked their walk and they were finished. I had no idea where I was going next but Tabitha invited me to live in her spare bedroom. It was something that should have excited me but I had lost the ability to smile.

I was the physical manifestation of apathy and indifference. A hardened shell of a former person. It wasn't Justin, it was the everything. It was the not knowing what would happen next or how long it would take to get there. I just didn't feel anything anymore but despair and every waking moment was a moment that I felt like I just wanted to be done with my life. The only time I could shut off that feeling was when I had just done a shot, or when I was obsessively hunting for a vein. The one thing those two had in common was their ability to help me vacate my reality. The vacation was always so temporary though, and then there I was again.

That attitude right there is exactly why Tabitha and I hit it off so well because we had that character trait in common. Neither one of us gave a shit about much of anything anymore. She asked me once, "You gonna go visit Justin in jail?

I just rolled my eyes. "He is dead to me. I bore easily."

She just said, "Well now I just love you, cause that's the best thing anyone has ever said to me." She laughed as she left the room.

Tabitha and I were a couple of hard ass bitches who also happened to be junkies and we didn't care about anyone or anything except getting high. We also watched each other's backs. She was a lesbian but she had a girlfriend. Our friendship had nothing to do with that kind of love. We bonded through darkness, despair, drugs and depression.

Over time we adopted the nickname junkie bitches from hell. That was because we took no shit and sometimes did some pretty despicable things to get our next high. I even had a nice little ball peen hammer that matched my purse. They looked so good together they should have been sold as a package deal. Our reputations preceded us, all I had to do was reach for the purse and people would hand over anything I wanted.

No one wanted the kind of trouble that came from crossing us. It kind of felt good to finally be in a position where people feared me instead of trying to take advantage of me. I really only had to take down one person for the word to spread, but then it spread like wildfire. I was a junkie bitch from hell. I had finally made something of myself.

Fifteen

The Junkie Bitches From Hell

*T*abitha and I were what you would call like-minded. I had developed a horrible outlook on life and hated the entire world. She had come into that hatred years before we met. She was very open about being a manic-depressive person and actually walked to the mental health clinic for regular electro shock treatments. Oftentimes when she was talking, she had a white foam building up in the corners of her mouth. One thing she was really good at doing was using her monthly social security check to get the rent paid but she wasn't so good at paying the rest of the bills.

Our home was like a drug store. We had a constant flow of traffic and constant flow of drugs. If anyone wanted anything they could just stop by our place, hang out for a short while and they would have it. The biggest suppliers in the area dropped by regularly and kept us stocked up. We rarely ate but when we did it would be due to food stamps or dumpster diving. Sadly enough, if I spent 100 dollars' worth of food stamps on groceries, they would all be gone in less than a day.

What the crazy thing was is that Tabitha and I hardly ever ate. It was all of the other people coming and going all day. I had a spot where I could go grab huge black garbage bags full of doughnuts. I would do that occasionally and then all the people coming and going from the house would get to enjoy a free continental breakfast.

One day the drug flow slowed down. We weren't sure how or what happened, but we laid around batting flies off our noses as we sweated to death. It was that old familiar carcass in the desert feeling. The withdrawals were a nightmare. Then a terrible revelation sprung Tabitha onto her feet. "We gotta pay our electricity bill today or they're shutting us off."

I sprung halfway up. "What? How do you know? What happened?"

"I fucking forgot!"

I laid back down. "What are we gonna do?"

Tabitha got up and put her shoes on. "We gotta go over there and get an extension."

"I'm starving, can you get food on the way?"

"I ain't got no money!"

I peeled myself up off of the bed and chased her out the door. "I'm coming!"

She just kept walking, feeling too shitty to speak. We took alleyways and different shortcuts to the electricity office. "Let's walk by the doughnut shop and see if we can get one." The barrels that usually had all the fresh doughnuts were empty. We walked past the dumpster in the alley and I looked down and saw it. I was so hungry that it practically glowed, it was a chocolate doughnut. The dumpster had been emptied yet this one beautiful and flawless chocolate doughnut sat at the bottom, carefully resting on a clean piece newspaper – like a Christmas present that had been left there for me.

The inner walls of the dumpster were black with soot and grime but the chocolate doughnut, resting on the clean newspaper, looked absolutely flawless. I couldn't get to it without getting the black goo all over me but that doughnut. I had to have it. I was absolutely starving and it was resting all perfectly as if on a platter, staying clean, while it waited for me. "You're not actually gonna eat that shit are you?" Tabitha interrupted my doughnut drool.

"I wish I could get to it without touching the walls – look how nasty they are."

"Alright, I guess we're doin' this. I'll hold your feet."

"Yasssss, that's perfect!" I hoisted myself up onto the front wall of the dumpster, Tabitha grabbed my ankles and lowered the front half of my body down like a see saw.

Just as I got my hands on the doughnut, I heard a window slide open above, "Hey! Get outta there!"

Tabitha laughed. "You got it?"

"Yes, lift me out." She hoisted me back up and I was on my feet. I held the doughnut towards the man in the window. He was a fireman, I guess the windows behind the doughnut shop led to the fire station, learn something new every day. "We're done!"

He looked at the doughnut. "You're not actually gonna eat that, are you?"

I laughed at him and took a bite. Tabitha laughed and snatched a piece for herself, then we waved at him and ran off to the electricity office. I never saw myself being able to see beauty in a chocolate doughnut that sat at the bottom of such a nasty, filthy, black dumpster but hunger is a funny thing. I couldn't see anything but beauty in that doughnut. I ate it and I enjoyed it.

Once we arrived to the electricity department, Tabitha went from person to person trying to get an extension. They were saying no and refusing to let her talk to a supervisor. She finally hollered at the lady she was talking to, "You people act like you're pumping this shit outta your god damned pussy!" The lady turned bright red and gave her five days to shut her up. I burst out laughing in the lobby and couldn't seem to stop laughing for the rest of the walk home.

On our way home, the cops stopped us. I thought it had something to do with either the electricity office or the doughnut, as the officer walked straight up to me. "June?"

"Um, yes?"

"Got any ID on you?" Then Officer Corbin pulled up and watched from his patrol car. I mean it looked like Corbin but he was different. I hadn't actually seen him in a while.

"Yeah, I do." I handed him my ID then smiled and waved at Corbin; he looked the other way.

The officer put me through a sobriety test, was looking up my nostrils,

112

checking my arms, which had track marks but they were days old. He called in my information and then said, "Turn around and put your hands behind your back."

"What? Why?"

"Just turn around and put your hands behind your back."

As he cuffed me he advised he was arresting me for being under the influence. He put me in the back seat of his patrol car, then hopped in and started driving us to the jail. Tabitha just stood on the sidewalk, dumbfounded. The officer said, "Corbin said to tell you hello."

I was taken to jail and drug tested. I passed because I hadn't used in several days. They let me go, but this was just the beginning. The jail was merely six blocks from home, but I was stopped along the way and put through the same thing every single time an officer saw me. I guess Corbin was making good on his promise. Maybe it was because of the stupid doughnut? Maybe it was because I was with Tabitha as she made a scene at the electricity office? I don't know, but something started happening and every time I was within eyeshot of a cop, I got stopped.

The worst one was the night I was riding with a friend across town. A cop started following us – for a really long time. As she pulled into her driveway he finally turned on his lights. Then he walked up to speak to her. "You can park and go inside – we're only interested in your passenger."

My stomach sank into my toes. I was terrified. It was the middle of the night and this cop had it out for me. A second cop car pulled up, I could only assume it was Corbin. I was arrested, once again for no reason. "Why in the hell do you keep doing this?" I shouted at the officer from the back seat.

He just looked at me in his rear-view mirror and smiled.

"You don't have any reason to arrest me!"

He just kept driving. Then he turned down a long dark road without a single street light in sight, and he pulled over.

Terror doesn't even effectively describe the feeling I had. Why in the world was this happening and what in the hell was going on? I watched him in the rear and side view mirrors. Then I saw the second patrol car pull up and the cop that I was riding with popped open the trunk. I could hear the officers talking back there and it was definitely Corbin. I couldn't make out what they were saying. I honestly thought they were going to kill me and bury me. Then they shut the trunk, the cop got back in, the other cop car flipped a U-turn and left.

The cop that was driving was doing something with his hands, he had something, it looked like a vial. He kept slapping it on the palm of his hand. As we pulled into the police station he advised me I was being taken into the police station to test the controlled substance they found on my person. Then he said the magic words, "Corbin said to tell you hi and that he hopes you're well."

I just rolled my eyes, pissed I was being set up and pissed I couldn't do anything about it.

To add insult to injury, they didn't even get the drug right. They said I was in possession of an ounce of Chyna White, which is a white powdery form of heroin. The only drug I ever used was methamphetamine, you'd think they'd at least get the drug right. I was thrown in jail, then at my arraignment there was another plot twist. The officer never filed the report, without a report the charges would have to be dropped.

The District Attorney requested an extension to give the officer time. The judge made it clear that the situation was despicably unprofessional but he granted a three-day extension, so I got to sit in jail another three days waiting. The three days came around and the charges still weren't filed. The judge gave a speech about the unprofessionalism of the Sheriff's Department and then he dropped all of the charges and let me go.

It was oddly familiar. Corbin always liked to throw me in jail and force me to get clean. He said it was to give me a safe place to stay, but it was really because he didn't want me to have access to any drugs. This time he found a way to put me in there longer. I can only assume they never filed the paperwork because his buddy that helped him orchestrate the whole thing may have been too nervous about following through? I don't know, but I was happy as hell to be out of there and I was totally tripping on Corbin. This was definitely a message, Corbin wanted me to remember his warning. He had eyes everywhere and I could be arrested for anything he pleased.

This whole situation started feeding my paranoia in an epic way. I would only go outside at night. I would only smoke in the dark if I had a way to hide it because the cherry end of the cigarette would expose my location. If anyone else tried to smoke in plain sight I'd rake them over the coals about it. I also had a system I was using to get around at night that involved hiding behind bushes and cars. If there weren't plenty of hiding spots between point A and point B, I just didn't go. This was my system and a lot of people I ran with thought it was hilarious, but it worked, so the joke was on them.

One time I met this couple, Cody and Tracy. They wanted me to help them acquire a larger amount of meth than we had on hand. I told them I can't be seen in public or I'd get stopped and busted. They had me lay down in the back of the car and took me to their place which was all the way across town. We made it there without incident. I made some phone calls and got them their stuff. They shared with me, that was always the deal for my services, I never sold my body, I just charged a fee for hooking people up with product and they could pay in cash or product.

I was trying to do a shot but having problems finding a vein. Cody offered to help me out. I stuck out my arm, and looked away at a magazine I was reading. I started feeling something unusual in my hand. I looked at Cody and he had this strange look of amazement on his face. I looked down and there was a huge bubble forming as he was injecting the meth. This doesn't ever happen. I had never seen anything like it, unless it was a miss, but missing a vein burns in an incredibly painful way. There was no burning, just bubbling and weird pressure. This, whatever was happening, was weird. "Stop!" He kept injecting, I pulled my hand away and put pressure on it. "What the fuck is wrong with you!"

"What? I figured the vein was just filling up."

"You mean blowing? You think it was gonna blow?"

"Did it hurt?"

"No, it felt weird. Just take me home."

On the drive back home, the back of my hand got hotter and hotter. There was a weird red spot forming. I couldn't stop thinking about the look on Cody's face when it happened. He should have stopped the injection but instead it looked like he was just seeing the most amazing thing he'd ever seen in his life. I suspected I had just let a total psychopath stick a needle into my hand. He was just flat out weird.

I started feeling a little sick so when I got home I laid down and actually fell asleep. When I woke it felt like my hand was literally on fire and it was frozen in some weird claw like position. It was the strangest thing, any time I tried to straighten out a finger, it would spasm and curl back up. It throbbed and hurt worse than any pain I had ever experienced in my life.

I filled the bathroom sink with ice, sat on the floor and put my hand in the sink. It only stopped throbbing when it was over my head, then I used popsicle sticks and tape to force my fingers straight. Tabitha saw me and demanded that I go to the emergency room. I felt too miserable to go anywhere so she walked around to neighboring houses and found me a ride.

Once there I was too paranoid to tell them what happened. The moment they saw the way my fingers would not extend without the popsicle sticks, they rushed me into a room. They told me it looked like I was probably going to lose my hand and the best way to help me was for me to tell them the truth. I told them enough of the truth for them to diagnose my hand. Cellulitis.

My judgmental doctor approached my bedside. "You have an extreme case of Cellulitis. You should have come in sooner, I honestly don't know if we can save your hand."

"This literally just happened! It's only been a few hours."

"No, that doesn't make any sense."

"It was IV drugs."

"I understand, that is the most common cause of this infection."

"He was injecting my hand, when some strange bubble formed." I showed the doctor the red spot and gave him a demo of how big the bubble was. "And now it's like this." I kind of painted a picture of myself as this guy's victim as I elaborated on what a psychopath he was. The doctor wasn't buying it, I could tell he knew I was a junkie. It was probably all the track marks that gave me away.

"Well, the best I can do is put you on IV antibiotics, the strongest dose we can, and then pray that it takes care of it. You should know up front that in addition to losing your hand, this condition can also kill you."

He left and a stupid nurse came in to run an IV. I call her stupid because the woman could not find a vein on me, I could do better than her. Then she came around to my infected side and wanted me to hang it down on the side of the bed so she could try there. I yelled at her, "It fucking hurts too much to hang it anywhere!" as I kept it up above my head to relieve the throbbing.

I was put on an IV antibiotic regimen that required me to return to the ER every day for three days. The doctor made sure I understood that if I didn't follow through I would absolutely, undoubtedly, lose my hand and he wasn't even sure that the treatment would work. On top of the IV I was put on a heavy-duty dose of oral antibiotics. I was a walking antibiotic.

I followed through with everything. The first IV 8 hours at the ER, the second one was a 6 hour IV and the third was a 4 hour IV.

During this time, I didn't use any more meth. There was a part of me that was physically disgusted with myself. The urge to use kept gnawing at me, but the thought of losing life and limb was a constant reminder of the disgust that kept me clean. I half expected Corbin to pay me a little visit at the hospital but luckily the hospital didn't drop a dime on me.

On my final treatment at the ER my doctor came into the room. "I'm discharging you early."

"Why? I'm doing everything you said."

"Because you're using here in the hospital and we can't have that."

"What in the hell are you talking about?"

He elaborated. "Your neighbor just walked out of the hospital because you were in the bathroom shooting up. I can't believe you did that here, we are trying to help you and you are making it too uncomfortable for other patients to get treatment."

I was already on edge from not using for several days so I pretty much came unglued and demanded a drug test, which I passed. I still didn't think they believed me, but they finished my treatment and let me know to follow up with my regular doctor instead of with them.

I was really pissed. I was going through hell trying to do the right thing while everyone I knew was using around me, and even while clean I got accused of using. This gave me the permission I needed. I walked home from the hospital and immediately grabbed a needle. As I was preparing the shot, I was plagued by this nagging feeling that I wasn't in control anymore. It was a momentary lapse of reason, resolved by the rush of the drugs.

Sixteen

The Rubber Room

~⚭⚭~

Something about methamphetamine shifts life and the world into high gear. It must be the fact that speed turns everything up, while turning everything off at the same time. Months had passed since the hand incident and luckily, I still had it. My needle obsession was at an all-time high and now that I had a room to call my own, I had a dresser to call my own. The top drawer was full of bloody spoons and needles. I knew it was disgusting, I knew it was sick, but I was too far gone to care.

My situation with local law enforcement had not improved at all and I was exhausted from all of the effort to evade them. So naturally, I dropped my guard and ended up arrested. Here's what happened. I went to the store in broad daylight for cigarettes. Then I was walking back to the house, and just as I was reaching the front yard I saw a cop car coming. My standard instinct was to hop over the fence and vanish into the house.

But, I just stood there. I was tired. I just stood there and let them arrest me. This time they said I had a warrant, but hey, there was always a garden variety of excuses to arrest me, anytime I saw a cop I knew I was going to jail. I seemed to draw them to me like a magnet, which made it kind of taxing to live the life I lived. This was very familiar to me, until what happened next; had I known sooner, I'd have run when I had the chance.

During the booking process, the jail staff looked at my arms, covered in bruises, track marks and I had an abscess on my forearm from missing a vein. It was a pretty big one. Of course, Corbin was standing there for the embarrassing expose. "Jeeze June, whatcha been doing to yourself?"

I rolled my eyes and looked down at the floor as he took pictures of my arms.

The jailer looked closer and rubbed the abscess with her index finger. "We can't accept her without medical clearance first."

"Come on, can't you just send her to your infirmary here?"

She laughed at him. "You wish."

"Come on, June, let's go to the hospital."

"I'm not going to any hospital!"

"You are in custody and will go where you're told."

Corbin drove me to the hospital as I plotted a way to manipulate the situation. By my summation of the situation, I could refuse medical treatment and then they would have to release me. So, when we got to the hospital, they checked me out and of course it was the same hospital I'd been to more than once.

The doctor examined my arms. "I'm gonna need to find out what's inside of the lump. I'll numb the area first." He used a small syringe to inject something into the area for numbing.

Then he stepped in with a HUGE syringe and shoved it right into the center of the lump in my arm, and it was painful. "Ouch, you fucking asshole!"

Doctor Asshole smiled at me, he actually smiled at me as he snidely said, "It's hard to numb an abscess. Sorry." Then he walked off like the asshole he was.

I laid there, with my eyes closed, waiting. Corbin was sitting in a chair just outside of the hospital room. The doctor returned and I flat out told him, "I refuse medical treatment."

He stepped over to me. "You can't be serious. There's an infection in your arm that, if left untreated, will result in a loss of the arm – it's well on its way to cellulitis."

"I don't care."

"I'm telling you that you will lose your arm if you don't get treatment, and you just don't care?"

I gave him a dirty look. "No."

He stepped out of the room and Corbin came in. He walked over, and pulled a chair up to the side of the bed. "You have to let them help you."

I stared up at the ceiling. "No."

"Listen, you can do this the easy way, or the hard way. You're in custody, this really isn't an option."

"They can't touch me without my permission."

"They can declare you incompetent to make your own decisions, and you clearly are."

"No, I'm not."

The doctor returned to the room. "The test results show it is a Staph infection. Do you know what that is?"

I ignored him and stared at the ceiling as he continued to try and scare me. "It will develop into blood poisoning and kill you."

Corbin spoke up again. "You're getting treated. Do I need to handcuff you to the bed?"

I was so tired of this, I honestly felt like I could pass out at any moment. I just wanted them to shut up and leave me alone. I closed my eyes. "So, IV antibiotics?"

"No, we actually need to cut it out."

"Great."

Corbin touched my hand. "I'll stay with you, let's get this done."

"Fine."

The nurse stepped in with some pain meds that she was going to give me through the IV. I was somewhat wrapped up in self-disgust at the moment and actually did not want any IV drugs. "Can I have a pill instead of injection?"

Everybody in the room seemed pretty surprised, and the nurse smiled at me. "Sure," she said, then left and got me pills. I should have asked why there weren't cookies and Kool Aid since everyone wanted to treat me like I was a god damned child.

The surgery took a long time and was kind of scary. It was the first surgery I had ever had. The doctor had this weird shield over his face, and used some weird irrigation thing to clean out the inside of my forearm. I silently cried a little. I normally didn't cry about anything, having shut down those emotions long ago, by poking holes in myself. The only real emotion I seemed to have left was rage. But, this day something new surfaced, it must have been the exhaustion and the painkillers.

The ride back to jail was a blur but I remember the booking process. The strangest thing happened to me. As I was standing there answering her questions I literally fell out of myself, then stood back up. Her and I looked at each other in an awkward moment of silence, as she knew something strange had happened too. I had never been successful at Astral Projection but in that exact moment I knew that was exactly what had happened. It must have been a result of my exhaustion, and the painkillers but that shit was crazy. I decided to sit down before I fell down - body, spirit and all.

The next thing I remember I woke up on the greenish colored floor of a strange room. There was a hole in the floor for peeing, and cameras everywhere. It was the rubber room. I was in the damned rubber room. I became nauseated, a friend of mine had died in that room less than six months earlier. Others had died in there too, I could not believe I was in the rubber room. I heard a voice talk to me over the speaker. "Are you feeling ok?"

I looked around at the cameras. "I need to pee." I looked at the hole in the floor and was totally humiliated by the idea that they were actually going to make me pee in that hole like an animal.

"Hold on, we'll come and get you."

Relieved, I sat up and steadied myself. I was really confused. I had lost a lot of time. A nice male officer showed up and opened my cell. "Can you walk?"

I shakily worked my way up onto my feet and walked out – following him to the bathroom. "Now that you're awake I'll get you moved to a new cell right away."

"How did I get in there?"

"You don't remember?"

I shook my head.

"You walked in."

"Really?"

He opened a door. "Here you go, take all the time you need." I stepped into a private bathroom. While I peed I started to move the gauze on my arm and then stopped. I wasn't ready to see it. Once finished I stepped out and he walked me back.

"It'll probably take me a couple of hours to get you moved. I want you to know, I don't agree with you being in the rubber room but now that I know you don't remember how you got there, I'm glad we did. It's for your own safety, we've been monitoring you the whole time, making sure you're ok." He opened the door and guided me back in. "I'll go get you a pillow and some extra blankets."

"Ok."

I walked to the back of the cell and sat in the corner. I was so disgusted with myself I didn't even know what to think. I tried to remember walking into this cell but couldn't. I sat there thinking about my friend who died in there and teared up a little imagining how horrible that must have been for him. While the officers watched him on the cameras and did absolutely nothing to help him.

A little while later a nurse showed up. She had medications for me, along with a bucket. "We need you to start soaking the wound four times a day for aftercare." She removed the gauze and looked at my arm. She glanced around the cell with a look of disgust on her face, as I struggled to avoid looking at my arm. "I'll be right back." Just a few minutes later she showed up with a wheelchair and other helpers and they moved me to a hospital bed cell. "This is more like it," she said as she got me into the bed.

She then set up a table and chair just outside of the room and guided me out there. She guided me through the steps of soaking my arm in Epsom salts and I finally had to look at it. The wound was partially covered in gauze, I could see there was a large hole and there was a wick sticking out of it, similar to the wick of a candle. She explained that the wick was there to draw out poisons. She removed it, and it stung. Then we soaked it. We did this every four hours as she gave me my antibiotics. "I'm going to get you released, you need to be home so you can recover properly."

She was a woman of her word, I soon went to court and was released on my own recognizance really quickly with a recommendation of Drug Diversion. I didn't pay a lot of attention to what they were saying but I heard enough to know I was supposed to not use drugs, I was supposed to go to the Probation Office to check in, etc. I was just happy as hell to be free.

I went back home and told Tabitha my story of woe. She offered me a hit, I passed. I laid around in my room, tripping on what I had done to myself, and wondering if I should try this drug diversion stuff. I was kind of feeling like I should, so I tried going to one of the meetings at the Substance Abuse office. It was like old home week in there, I knew everyone, some of my old boyfriends were even in there. The counselor asked me to leave though because it was an aftercare group for people who had a certain amount of clean time.

Only a few days had passed and there was some really good meth at the house. I said, "Fuck it" and decided to use again. The only good vein I had left was where the surgery had happened, and I still had a big hole in my forearm. I just decided to use the vein again, but about an inch above the hole. It worked out and nothing bad happened so I was back at it again. Over the following months my paranoia about the cops was at a record high, especially because I was now absconding from drug diversion.

I had exhausted the veins in my arms by this point and had taken to shooting up in some odd places. I had a vein in one of my breasts that I used occasionally, I had become well versed at shooting in my neck, but the easiest veins I had were in my legs. I really liked the legs because cops never looked there if I was questioned.

One night I was so wired I that ended up riding somewhere with a complete stranger, to my friend Katty's house up in the mountains. This place was so obscure that they only had one gas pump in town. We went there to see if they wanted to buy some drugs, because we were both wired and didn't really consider much of anything else. Everything was going well until the guy I rode with randomly left, with my syringe in his car.

Katty didn't have a car, plus it was the middle of the night. So, I was stuck in the middle of nowhere with lots of good drugs and no way to use them. Out of desperation, I found an old, bent needle in the bottom of my bag. I rinsed it really good and tested it. Surprisingly, it was fully functional. The vein in my calf was huge, so I decided to use the bent needle in that one. It worked at first, but then the needle stopped working halfway through the shot.

I tossed it out. I hadn't slept in days and sitting there in the dark trailer was making my eyes heavy. I finally closed them for a minute and ended up passing out. When I woke up my leg was throbbing and had grown at least five times its normal size. It was just like what happened to my hand, but on a much larger scale. I was in so much pain that I couldn't even walk.

Katty asked me what was wrong, I showed her my leg. "I was desperate and used an old needle I had."

"Ah shit, we gotta get you the hospital."

"No hospitals, please, the cops will be all over the place! They know my face, I can't go there."

"We'll go to the hospital on the other side of the county. Do they know you there?"

"No, but what if the hospital calls the cops?"

"Just go in under my name." She ran to her purse and pulled out her Medi-Cal card. "Use this to check in, you'll be good." She talked me into it and even found a ride there. Once inside of the ER I couldn't shake the paranoia. There were literally cops everywhere. This was a different ER in a different town but it didn't matter. It felt like all eyes were on me and the paranoia won over the pain. We left.

Once back at her place she found some unfinished antibiotics and I started eating them like candy. It took a couple of days but the swelling finally subsided enough for me to walk again, and she helped me find a ride into town. I was too paranoid and embarrassed to go to the ER so I went to the walk-in clinic. The doctor advised that the antibiotics saved my leg but I may not be out of the woods yet. He drew circles around the injection site, loaded me up with high powered antibiotics and I was supposed to check in once a week. I was disgusted with myself, again. I could not believe what I did. I made up my mind to stay away from Tabitha's and get my life together.

I went to the 90-year-old man Charlie's house. He was someone I had many interactions with over the years. He was a little bit of a pervert but since he could barely walk I really wasn't worried about it. I used him from time to time if I was starving, or needed a phone, or a ride, or whatever. I also helped him when I could.

This old man was still going to nightclubs on the weekends. The extent of his sex life was all hands off. He liked what he called a visual aid. Rather than looking at an adult magazine, he liked to have an actual woman lay down naked in front of him and then he masturbated while touching her thighs. Being at his old age he was used to paying a fee to whomever he could get to do it.

I had stayed at his place in the past and I always made it clear that I didn't do that kind of thing, but, since he was helping me out I would help him out. My help consisted of contacting one of my friends who was a prostitute. I'd make the introductions then take off. One time I charged him a fee for making the introductions. Aside from the annoying propositions, Charlie was harmless and I really needed a place off the meth grid to rest, heal, and take my antibiotics. So, I knocked on his door.

He welcomed me inside, let me cook myself something to eat and then propositioned me. "I won't even touch you, I just need you to take off your clothes and lay down in front of me."

"I've told you a bunch of times before, I don't do that."

"I'll pay you!" He pulled a twenty out of his pocket. "Look, do you need more?"

"Ugh, why do you have to be such a pervert, Charles?"

"I always help you, you always come here when you need stuff and I'm tired of it."

"I always find you a girl when you ask, and when's the last time I called you?"

He ignored me and walked into his room. I was in a weird place. I had no idea what I was doing or where I was going to go next but it seemed like every time I disgusted myself with the needle, I lost a little bit more of me. I was in a spiral and then I just did it. This was one thing I had held true to for years, I did not sell my body. I'd had about enough of that when I was thirteen and wasn't given a choice. I wanted out of the life I had been living so badly that I said to hell with it, at least it's different. I walked into his room, took of my clothes and laid down in the bed the way he wanted me to. Legs spread, towards him. He touched my inner thighs, and looked at my body while he masturbated. It was awkward, and a new place of self-disgust for me. He handed me two twenties. I put on my clothes and went back to the couch. As I sat there, the weight of what just happened was too much to bear.

I got up, walked out, and headed straight to Tabitha's house. A dealer was there with some of the best dope in town, I handed him the money I'd just made, got some dope, and went into the bathroom. I put it all into the spoon for a 100-unit injection.

I wouldn't dare touch my leg veins with all that I had going on down there. The arm was pretty sketchy too. I was on a downward tailspin, so I put a bottle of nail polish in my mouth, and blew on it really hard to make the veins in my neck pop out. There was a part of me hoping that I would overdose. I did the shot, it was pretty awesome, and suddenly like magic all of my problems went away again.

This one was a two-week run. I was shooting in my neck exclusively. After not sleeping for so long, I was back in the bathroom, looking for the vein, and almost made myself pass out from pressing on my neck veins for too long. Cause you know me, it's no fun unless I spend hours stabbing myself.

It felt like something was crawling on the back of my leg. I remained focused on the mirror while using my other foot to swipe at it. Then it got worse, like multiple things were crawling on my leg. I finally stopped the neck obsession to look at my leg. There was a large black spot on the back of my leg, with a hole in it, and this orange puss substance was oozing out. There were also black streaks spanning the calf area, it was shocking enough that I dropped the needle, sat down on the side of the bathtub and stared at my leg.

I went to Tabitha.

"Girl, you need to go to the hospital." She walked over to the cabinet under the sink. "But since I know you ain't going…" Reaching into the cabinet under the sink, she pulled out a box of Epsom salt. "Soak." She drew the bathtub and poured a bunch of salt in. "This will draw out the poisons." Laughing at me," she said, "Hope you don't lose your fucking leg."

I was speechless. I had really, really, screwed up. Instead of taking the antibiotics I was just using, using, using, using, to my own peril. I knew I needed to stop but I just couldn't. I soaked my leg and kept going but I couldn't use my neck anymore and I was back to the epic vein hunting.

One day we had company, she was supposedly a former nurse. She offered to help me find a vein. She had already poked me twice and was going for the third try. I don't really know what it was but something washed over me, as if something moved through me, and I burst into uncontrollable tears.

She stopped and pulled the needle out. "What's wrong?"

I sobbed. I think it was the first time I sobbed in, well, I don't know how long.

"I don't know. It's like I don't want to do this anymore but I can't not do it."

"Honey, that's Jesus talking to you."

My tears turned to rage. "No it fucking isn't! Are you gonna do this or not!"

She quietly resumed and gave me the injection.

Later that night, Tabitha burst into my room. "The cops are at the door!"

"No fucking way! What do they want?"

"How the fuck should I know?"

"Is Corbin out there?"

"I don't fucking know! Go into the bathroom!"

I stared at the top drawer of my dresser and focused in on it as I felt all of the air leave the room. It was going to be Corbin, it was going to be him and his buddies. They were going to see how disgusting I was. That drawer, that very drawer, held the truth of what I had become. A rock bottom junkie who held onto bloody spoons and needles. What in the hell was I going to do? I just couldn't do it, I couldn't face them, I couldn't let them see, I had to escape.

I rushed into the bathroom, locked the door, and started filling up the tub. I stripped down, I knew male police officers couldn't barge in on a naked woman, I figured this would buy me some time while they waited for a female officer to arrive. Then I grabbed a shaving razor, broke off as much of the plastic I could, sank into the bathtub and began cutting my wrist.

I could hear Tabitha shouting and furniture being thrown around. I was desperate to bleed out before they figured out where I was. I could not allow them to find me, I couldn't let them see what I had become. The blood, it just wasn't flowing fast enough so I cut more, and deeper. "Hurry up and die," I muttered to myself. I was all in, all the way, and there was no way they were taking me out of there alive. BOOM! BOOM! BOOM! Tabitha shouted, "You can come out now, they're gone!"

Seventeen

The Metamorphosis

*T*his was an indescribable moment. My insanity was temporarily arrested as my sanity took over. Shockingly enough, I guess there was still some sanity within me but it had been on a long, long, vacation. I looked down at myself and all I saw was blood, my blood. I was encapsulated in it. The effect of blood in water was overwhelming as I laid there submerged in mine.

I stared at my body, riddled with holes, bruises, scars, and lumps. What had I become? I looked up and for the first time I noticed that the ceiling was covered in little droplets of blood, the floors, the walls. It was from the countless hours of poking a vein, pulling out the needle, pushing out the air, and poking again.

I knew in that moment that I had completely lost my mind, myself, my soul. I wasn't even me anymore, I was a shell of a woman with nobody home inside. The idea that I'd just cut myself repeatedly to avoid letting the cops see how sick I was really resonated within me. It was like being raped, all over again.

This wasn't me, how could this be me? I got up, drained the tub, reached for my clothing, and saw that my clothing was riddled with the same specks of blood. I was too ashamed to let Tabitha know what had happened in that bathroom. I wrapped my wrist in toilet paper and walked to my room. She was pressed up against the bathroom door and nearly fell in when I opened it. She followed me to the room, telling me what happened. Her voice droned on, I was in a moment.

I started looking at my other clothes and noticed the same little droplets of blood on those too, I opened the drawer to my bloody spoons and needles. "I thought for sure they were going to find this."

Tabitha scrunched up her nose. "Ew, welcome to my nightmare," and she laughed. That was what I loved the most about her, she called it like she saw it and could she have called it anything else? I actually laughed with her, and although I had just been through an ordeal I would never tell her about, she still managed to make me laugh.

I waited for her to finish talking and then I left. I felt like a ghost, as I floated away from the house at odds with the entire universe. I knew I had lost my mind and I wondered if it was too far gone to find it again. I couldn't see any way out of hell. I walked straight to the hospital for some proper bandages, I did not care if the cops stopped me. I no longer cared much about anything – numb, indifferent, and completely lost.

I looked at the young female doctor and envied what I saw in her. As she cleaned the cuts on my wrist she asked me how old I was, and answering her made me cry, uncontrollably as I choked out the words, "Twenty-five."

I left there and walked to the substance abuse program. I sat down in a chair in front of one of the counselors and shouted at them, "I haven't been here because you guys said I can't come here loaded! But I can't stop using! What the hell kind of a place is this if a person has to be clean to get in here! I mean, isn't helping people get clean what this place is supposed to be about? Fucking racket!"

She smiled at me and motioned for me to follow her into the group room. "Have a seat."

She proceeded to start the group. "Today we are talking about step one, Powerlessness." As the group proceeded she explained what powerlessness was. Finally! An EXACT description of how I had been feeling. It's like this woman had been spying on me, or could read my mind or something, because in my heart I definitely wanted to stop but I just kept using anyways. You see, in my heart I know what I'm doing is wrong but it's like my hands have a mind of their own.

That is exactly what powerlessness means.

During the group another staff member opened the door and made me follow her to an office. "June, you can't be here loaded. Nobody else gets to and neither do you."

"I need help, if I could get clean on my own I wouldn't need this place!"

"You better figure it out cause you can't come here, and our waiting list for residential treatment is long. You'll be waiting months."

"God, you're a bitch."

I got up and stormed out.

As I was walking home I prayed for the first time in my life. It was really simple, "God, if You're real and You give a shit about me at all. It's time to let me die, or help me find a different life. Because I can't go on living this way and You keep making me! I keep trying to die and You won't let me! I try to change my life, and it's impossible! I have nowhere to go, I can't trust anyone. And any God who would make me stay alive and suffer is just cruel. You either hate me or You just aren't real. But if You are real, and You do give a shit about me, either help me or put me out of my misery. Amen."

Later that night an old friend tracked me down, actually, several old friends tracked me down. They said a man called them and told them it was an emergency, I needed to call him back immediately. "Well did he say what it was about?"

"No!"

This is what I kept hearing from everyone who came knocking, and honestly, I was working towards another shot so the knocks were getting really annoying. They gave me his number so I found a phone and called him back. He introduced himself, he was a counselor at the substance abuse program and he informed me that he had a free bed for me at a residential treatment center for 45 days.

Dumbfounded. I was completely, unequivocally dumfounded. I did not know what to think or say or do. Was this some kind of immediate and miraculous answer to my prayer? I suspected so but I was afraid. I was afraid to be too hopeful. To be hopeful meant to be uplifted, and the higher a spirit rises the harder it falls. I was too excited to ignore it. This, this was finally my way out of hell.

"Where?"

He gave me the address with a strong warning. "We pulled some serious strings to get you in there because your counselor said it's an emergency."

"It's only a five-minute walk from where I'm at, I'll be there."

"Good luck and check in with us when you're done."

I hung up and walked back home. I told Tabitha, "This is only temporary cause I have to take a break, I'll be back as soon as I can."

"I can't believe you're leaving me! You're the best roommate I ever had."

"You save a shot for me cause I'm coming back," I told her, and I meant it. I wanted her to save my room for me, I wanted to know that when I came back she would still be there.

"I promise, the room is always yours."

I packed some clothes into grocery bags, then I stopped, grabbed a syringe and a small baggie of meth that I still had. I stashed it all in my sock. I knew it was wrong but I was too afraid to walk out of the house without it. As I was walking out the door, Tabitha ran up to me and gave me a huge hug. "Don't come back! Get your life together! You can do a lot better than this hellhole."

She made me cry, I couldn't believe we were saying goodbye. I said, "But we're the junkie bitches from hell."

"No, that's me," she replied as she wiped a tear from her eye. "I've been really fucking scared for you." She looked down at my leg. "This is exactly where you need to go, but my door is always open to you anyways."

As I walked to the treatment center I realized I was making a huge mistake. So, I turned around and went back to the house. I walked into the house, headed straight into my room and sat down on the bed. I pulled the drugs and syringe out of my sock. I held the syringe in my hands and stared at it. This tiny little thing had been ruling my life for years. This tiny little thing had completely stolen my identity.

I got up, walked over to my dresser, placed it in the nightmare drawer, placed the baggy of meth into the drawer, slowly slid the drawer closed, then walked out of hell house to embark on a collision course with my future – whatever that was.

When I arrived in front of the building I was really surprised about the location. This was a building I passed by every single day. I had sold drugs just outside of the parking lot. It was really hard to process the fact that this was a residential treatment center. I paused outside of the front doors and sat down on a planter – watching a butterfly feed on the flowers. It took me back to the butterfly I saved when I was a kid. My first real friend in this world was a butterfly. I hadn't seen a butterfly in so long that the sight of this one was completely mesmerizing. I have to confess, I did kind of wonder if it was a sign. I hoped it was a sign, I got up and walked into the treatment center. Absolutely terrified.

Eighteen

The Purple Dinosaur

I'm not sure how I got so far into the darkness....
    Maybe it was the drugs?
    Maybe it was the needle?
  Maybe it was the everything?

I walked in and was surprised by what I saw. It looked like a bar, but the imagery on the walls told another story. I was a little uncertain of whether or not I was in the right place. The first person I saw inside was an elderly woman, she popped out of an office and greeted me. "Checking in?"

I didn't know what to say. "I was told to be here today."

"Probation?"

She confused me, and I just stared at her.

"Who told you to come?"

"The guy at the substance abuse place."

"Ok, have a seat. One of the counselors is gonna have to meet with you first so we can make sure you're serious."

"Oh."

She walked up to a dining room table and pulled out a chair. "Sit."

I walked over and sat down. My nerves shifted into high gear right then as I suddenly didn't know if I was gonna get to stay. It sounded like a test. Nobody ever believes me or understands the words that come out of my mouth. I mean, sometimes I wonder if I'm really talking or if I'm just hallucinating that I'm talking, like that time when those weird door people came out of the…

"Hi, June?"

My crazy mental rant was interrupted by a woman standing in front of me. She had a very warm and welcoming smile on her face. "I'm Beth, the Program Coordinator here. Walk with me, let's get you checked in."

She reached out for a handshake but I just stared. I really wasn't intentionally trying to be rude but I just didn't like to shake hands, or touch, or anything. She dropped her hand and looked around at my grocery bags. "Are these your things?"

I nodded.

She grabbed my bags, I reacted for a second, she saw the reaction and put her hand on my shoulder. "It's ok." She smiled at me and lifted her other arm to point to where we were going. "Let's go to my office." The moment we started walking I began to sob. She put an arm around me. "What are these tears about?"

I just shrugged my shoulders and cried.

"Some people describe the fear of their first time in treatment like having a bird in their stomachs, like butterflies, but bigger." She laughed and wiped a tear away from her own face as she cried with me. "Is that how it feels?"

I nodded my head.

"Just relax and breathe."

This was all so much to take in and I was so scared. I had no idea what was to come, or if I would even be allowed to stay. I didn't know there was going to be test of some sort, but I really, really, wanted to stay. It was a hot day out and I was wearing a long-sleeved flannel. She sat down beside me. "Can I see?"

She placed her hand on my arm. I didn't want to, I shook my head and pulled my arm away. She looked at me with a sincerity I had never seen before. "If this is going to work."

I pulled up my sleeve and extended my arm to her. She used her fingers to touch all of the marks and bruises. She traced my arm with her index finger then smiled at me. "If you want to stay you have to follow this one rule. Well, there's other rules too, but this is first and foremost."

"Ok."

"No more long sleeve shirts."

"But, I don't want anyone to see my arms."

"It's time to stop hiding."

"Ok, but, what if other people say stuff?"

"If anyone says a word to you I want you to tell me." She rubbed a lump on my arm, similar to lumps I'd had in the past. "Have you had a doctor look at this?"

"No, but it's fine. I've had problems in the past, this one is fine."

"Well, rule number two is, you have to go see a doctor, today. In fact, I want you to call and make an appointment, right now." She handed me a phone book and a phone.

I hated that I had to go in and see a doctor about this, again, but I did. They got me worked in right away and Beth arranged a ride for me. I hadn't seen this particular doctor since he drew the circle on the back of my leg. I told him what ended up happening, and he looked at that too. It had healed enough that there was a very thin layer of skin over it. "You're really lucky you didn't lose that leg." Then he looked at my arm and he agreed that it wasn't infected, yet. He recommended warm compresses and antibiotics.

Later that night, while I was smoking with the other women, one of them pointed at my arm and said, "Hey, what's that?" Some of the other women standing around started looking at my arm too. I got really pissed, I didn't want people staring at my arms.

"Mind your own business!"

"There's a red line, June, you have an infection, a bad one."

"No, I fucking don't!"

"I'm telling you, that needs to be checked out."

"Leave me alone, it's fine."

"I used to be a nurse, I know what I'm talking about." Then she marched into the building and ratted me out.

A few minutes later Kim – one of the staff members - came out to look at it and suddenly there was a big scene about my arms, which was exactly why I wanted to keep them covered up in the first place. She took me to the emergency room. On the way there she asked me if I had a preference of hospitals. I divulged that I was embarrassed to go to the one nearby because I had been there so many times for this kind of thing. I requested the Catholic hospital which was just a little further away.

I had no idea that divulging the reason for my preference was such a mistake, until she said, "Imagine how good it will feel to tell them you're clean now," and that's exactly where she took me. Ugh, the frustration was unreal. I hated every single person at this treatment center!

Once inside it was confirmed, I had blood poisoning. It had already traveled up a good portion of my arm, they traced it to my armpit and suspected it was already very close to my heart. I was advised that it may already have gone too far to stop, as the very kind female doctor softly spoke to me. "This is a life-threatening situation."

I rolled my eyes in the irony of it all. "Can't you just cut it out?"

"Um, no. The infection has entered your bloodstream. Cutting out the source of the infection is secondary at this point. If we can't stop the infection in your bloodstream, it will kill you. And...."

I interrupted her, "I could lose my arm?"

She smiled at me. "At this point losing your arm is the least of our worries, you are well on your way to losing your life. We are going to do the best that we can, we'll treat the blood poisoning and remove the source of the infection." She stepped away and then an army of nurses started fluttering around the room.

Nurses rushed around me to run the IV antibiotics but since I had tapped out all of the veins they were having a lot of trouble. I had tourniquets on both arms, and both legs. There were literally four nurses poking me at the same time. They were even trying my feet but not getting anywhere. The head nurse apologized to me. "I'm so sorry about this, we are probably going to have to go for an artery, I have a specialist coming up."

While I waited all I could think of was that prayer that seemed to have landed me in this situation. I asked God to help me or put me out of my misery. It seemed like He acted quickly and put me onto a new path but was it just some cruel joke? Was I seriously going to die anyways? Why offer me a new life just to take it away so quickly?

I knew while I was laying there that I may have finally done myself in and that I had found my way into treatment just a little too late. Then Kim asked me if I'd like to say the serenity prayer with her. "I don't know the serenity prayer." Just then the specialist walked in and went straight for my wrist.

He had an artery kit with him. "Sometimes I have luck in these really deep wrist veins but there's a lot of tendons and nerves here. You cannot move your hand, at all, or you will permanently damage your wrist and paralyze your hand. You see?" He rotated my hand around and showed me the tendons.

Kim stepped over to the left side of the bed and grabbed my hand. "Let me help you relax, just repeat after me." I gripped her hand as she spoke.

I repeated everything she said. "God, grant me the serenity, to accept the things I cannot change, the courage to change the things I can, and the wisdom to know the difference."

A total stranger, holding my hand and helping me through something that I normally had to go through alone, was a brand-new experience for me that made me feel, new. Then she kind of startled me as she shouted, "Look!"

I looked over and saw the specialist taping down the successful IV, the nurses all applauded, plus more people outside of the room. Which was really weird to hear but kind of made me feel all fuzzy at the same time as I felt important. I don't think I could ever remember feeling important, until this moment right here. I felt like a miracle had just transpired in that room and everyone around experienced it too. There was a joyous feeling in the air, so much different than any of my previous visits to this hospital that I wondered if I was dreaming.

The surgery went well but I had a brand-new gaping hole in my arm. I had to return for several days for IV antibiotics as they said that the infection was too severe for oral. They gave me a purple stuffed dinosaur for having a day clean and being in a treatment center. The whole experience, although it was very intense, was also very joyous at the same time. In the face of a tragic situation everyone was smiling and happy, including myself, and I had to admit. The stuffed animal was kind of special too.

Nineteen

Butterfly

A lthough there was a warm and fuzzy feeling in the air – no one forgot they were dealing with a hardcore junkie and there was a dilemma. I needed IV antibiotics for several days and running an IV had been quite an ordeal. They wanted me to go back to the treatment center, then return to the Emergency Room for my daily treatments. In some people's cases, they would just leave the IV PICC Line in so that they didn't have to run a new IV every day. In my case, the hospital felt it was too huge a liability.

The joyous mood in the room gave way to the cold hard truth, nobody trusted me. I can't say I blame them, I could literally wander off and get high at any moment. I never knew from one second to the next if I was going to get high or not. Kim really surprised me, "I think that June has made a choice and that we should trust that choice." I looked at Kim, quietly amused at her naivety.

My doctor looked at me. "It's not that I don't believe in you, it's just that with your history. Well, I think it's too much of a temptation." It was funny watching her, as she watched her words so carefully. What she said to me was really supportive, but what she said with her eyes was that she knew the odds of me staying clean for more than a day were really low. She definitely didn't suffer from the naivety of Kim, that Kim, nice as she was, put way too much trust in me.

Kim walked over to my doctor and handed her a business card. "We have staff around the clock, we will keep an eye on her."

My doctor looked at Kim, then looked at me, and gave in. "I'm just gonna need you to sign a release of liability." Then the doctor pointed out to me. "This doesn't work the way you might think it does, if you screw around with it you could really hurt yourself."

"I'm not gonna screw around with it, promise." I smiled at them, hoping they bought it.

Kim signed the release and I walked out of the hospital locked and loaded. It was like a free pass to use as much as I wanted to. All I would need to do is slide the needle into the little housing unit and voila! I couldn't believe how easy it would be and I got excited thinking of how simple it was and how much fun I could have. I was wondering when I should take off, and figured I could slip away later in the night, when Kim said, "I stuck my neck out for you and I'm probably going to get in trouble. Please don't run off."

My fantasy was rudely interrupted by a twinge of guilt; after all, her and I had just gone through a very intimate experience together. I turned towards her, smiled and said, "I won't." I was lying, I already had one foot out the door. Something plagued me though, it was the existence of God. I had just experienced a miraculous answer to my only prayer. I mean, even I could see that I had experienced a miracle, which was kind of a big deal because I did not allow myself to buy into any form of hope. That part of me died years ago, and it was hardened by years of self-torture and abuse.

Upon our return to the treatment center I tried to go upstairs to my room, but Kim had other plans for me. "I know you're tired, but there's an AA meeting going on and I want you to go to it."

"Why? I'm not an alcoholic."

"It's about the 12-steps - it doesn't matter what your drug of choice is, the message is still the same."

"But I'm tired."

"Just attend the speaker meeting and then you can go rest." Even though I already had one foot out the door, it was best to put on my most convincing act until I literally had my foot out the door. So, I begrudgingly complied.

I could hardly hear anything going on in the room, because everyone's voices were being drowned out by the sight of veins. Yes, veins. It was all I could pay any attention to. It seemed like everyone in that room had huge, healthy veins. I just stared at their veins and fantasized about getting high. I knew there was something sick and twisted about it so I tried to be subtle, and when a person I was staring at looked my way I would quickly shift my stare to someone else's veins.

My thoughts of shooting up were all I could hear. I didn't hear anything else in the meeting until the speaker's closing statement, because once we stood in a circle facing each other it was too hard to discreetly stare at anyone's veins. As we all stood there holding hands for the final prayer of the meeting the speaker said, "Just stick this out one day at a time, even if all you can think about is using, talk to someone about it, white knuckle it till tomorrow, it keeps getting better." Then the final prayer was said. There were about 50 people in the room, all holding hands and saying the exact same words at the exact same time.

"Our Father, who art in heaven, hallowed be thy name. Thy kingdom come, thy will be done, on earth as it is in heaven. Give us this day, our daily bread, and forgive us our trespasses, as we forgive those who trespassed against us. And lead us not into temptation, but deliver us from evil. For thine is the kingdom, the power, and the glory forever. Amen."

Then everybody squeezed each other's hands tighter and pumped as they shouted, "Keep coming back!"

I had never experienced such a thing. How did all of these people know the words to that? It was such a surreal experience that I actually stopped obsessing about using, and stopped staring at people's veins for the duration of that entire prayer.

There was an undeniable energy in the power of so many people praying together – hand in hand. It kind of brought tears to my eyes as I sat there and the wave of the miracle of the new life I had been given washed over me. I walked back over to the dining room area and told Kim I had been thinking about walking. She smiled, cried a little and gave me a hug. "Thank God you decided to stay." Then she put me on the Buddy System, which means she assigned me a chaperone, it was another female resident, Becky ."I'm giving you a buddy, what she's going to do is stay close to you so you can talk to her when you're struggling and if you need help it's her responsibility to tell the staff."

I would normally be pissed to have a chaperone following me around all the time, but this was a new day. This was a new me. I was surrendering to the power of the twelve-step program, because there was simply something magical happening in that building, and I very much wanted to be a part of it.

When I laid my head down that night I uttered my second prayer. "Thank you, thank you for answering me, I hope this works out." The next morning, I wandered downstairs and there was a woman there I hadn't met before. I was intimidated by her, she just looked like the kind of person who would judge me. I didn't feel comfortable being around her, I just knew I wasn't good enough. I managed to avoid her while getting my ride to the Emergency Room for my dose of IV antibiotics.

I paid close attention to how the nurse utilized the little contraption that was hanging out of my wrist. She unwrapped the gauze and removed the tape. Then she popped something off of the end, stuck a needle in and drew it back, I was being nosy, as I was very interested in learning how to use the PICC. "What's that you're doing there?"

She seemed on edge, like someone had prepped her for the junkie she was going to be treating that day. "Just getting it ready for the saline."

"Saline?"

"We use saline to make sure the IV is still good before we hook up the antibiotics."

"Oh." I was perplexed to hear that this wasn't a guarantee.

She confirmed it was good, then hooked me up to the bags and I laid there for hours. I tried to nap but I was too anxious. When it was over she taped and covered everything back down like Fort Knox, then called the treatment center and I was escorted back. I know they were all bending over backwards to help me but I have to admit I struggled with feeling like a prisoner, like I was on constant watch.

I had experienced a whirlwind of miracles in a very short time. I had experienced something that was nothing short of magical in that treatment center. I wanted to be a part of it but my addiction was constantly gnawing at me. My old life was trying to win me back, and I didn't know what I was thinking, buying into the hope that this place was pushing anyways. I made up my mind that as soon as I got back up to my room, I'd just grab my stuff and leave.

When I walked into the building, the scary lady I had been avoiding earlier cut me off at the door. "June?"

My heart sank, I had a million things running through my mind and the number one fear I had was that someone set me up for having done something, and I was in some kind of trouble. *What did I do that I didn't do, this time?*

"My name is Frances, I'm the executive director here." She extended her hand out to shake mine. "Oh, you probably can't shake right now. Can you?" She gently grabbed my hand and looked at my gauze wrapped wrist. "Can you come and have a seat at the table with me?"

"Sure, but whatever it is, I didn't do it." I followed her to the table, she pulled out a chair and turned to me with a look of amusement.

"I'm only here a couple of days a week and I like to meet all of my new residents face to face."

"Oh." I'm sure my cheeks were red as I sat down.

"Do you want a soda?"

I knew the soda machine required money, which I didn't have, so I respectfully declined. "No."

"Ok, I'll be right back."

She returned and sat two diet sodas down on the table. "Sorry about the diet soda, but we don't believe in sugary, caffeinated sodas around here." She popped her can open and nodded at the other one. "Go ahead, it's on me."

I couldn't resist an ice-cold soda, even if it was diet, so I drank it and she pulled out a box of Uno cards. "Have you ever played Uno?"

I smiled, I hadn't seen an Uno card in years. "Uh, wow, a long time ago." She started shuffling the deck.

"My card playing partner couldn't make it today, is there any way you could join me?"

I hesitated, I kind of had plans slipping out of that place but I wanted to be discreet about it. I supposed I could play a game of cards with her then disappear later. I guess I had forgotten how much fun Uno is, because I ended up sitting there with her for a long time. My wrist started to ache a little from playing cards but that was ok because I was soaring on the inside.

We talked about my situation, what I had done to myself and how I almost died at the hospital because I had destroyed my veins too much for the IV and she just told me, "My veins are really bad too and I never used a drug a day in my life. Alcohol was my poison." She just completely deflated the shame I felt about myself.

I felt a deep level of acceptance from the lady in charge of the treatment center and it made me feel like I was home. There was no judgement, only a gesture of love and she didn't even want anything in return except to play Uno. She bought me more sodas and I learned about the foundation of the treatment center.

It was simple. "This was founded by my late husband. He was an alcoholic and he drank right here in this building. It used to be a bar with a motel up above and a lot of dirty dealings in the basement. One day, he went upstairs to one of the motel rooms and detoxed. Then, he went down to the bar and watched everyone drink but he remained sober. As other people reached the bottom of their alcoholism, he would offer to do the same for them. They would go upstairs with him, get sober, and then for class they all came downstairs and watched the other people drink. That's how I got sober. Over time we took over the building and turned it into what it is today. We left the bar as a reminder. When he died I took the reins. I'm only here on borrowed time, by all rights I should have died years ago, but God spared me so that I could carry the message to people like you."

She kind of made me cry a little. "Thank you," I choked out.

"Oh no, sweetie, don't thank me. I am just a messenger. It's God you should be thanking. Anyways, we believe in a cold turkey detox here, sugar and caffeine are a drug. We only have decaffeinated coffee and diet sodas. Once a week you get ice cream but that is to allow you to experience treatment without the aid of any mood or mind-altering substances. We allow smoking, of course, because nobody would stay if they couldn't smoke," she added with a laugh, "but no sugar or caffeine, it can get you kicked out of the program."

"Ok."

"Also, the 12-step program was founded by Alcoholics Anonymous. You're going to find that the literature is all AA literature, and the only support groups you are allowed to go to for the first 15 days are AA. The reason for this is simple, it is the basic foundation of the 12-step program. It's more developed and members of AA have been in recovery a lot longer than most people in Narcotics Anonymous. The 12 steps can be applied to every single situation you have in life, so just apply it to your drug addiction. When you're ready for NA literature your counselor will give it to you." On those final words, she got up and pointed at the clock. "Well, it's time for me to go."

It was 5 p.m. Her and I had been sitting there for hours. I couldn't believe how much time had passed and in all of that time I never once thought about using, I wasn't staring at her veins, I wasn't thinking about running away. That woman was the nicest person I had ever met in my life. I was all in, again. I went up to my room and took a nap.

A short while later I ended up wandering out of the treatment center. I was so powerless over my addiction, that even though my heart said no, my body always said yes. I told myself I was just going to visit Tabitha because I wanted to tell her about how cool the program was but I wasn't going to use. Suddenly, I went from walking, to injecting meth into my IV PICC. I wasn't even at Tabitha's house. I had lost time and I had absolutely no understanding of where I was or how I got there.

One thing was certain though, I had just fucked up and used again. I felt my world of darkness and despair crashing down on me again as I walked back to the treatment center. I knew I'd never get away with it, I knew these people who were so kind to me were going to make me leave. As I approached the building I finally found Tabitha. She was standing outside of the treatment center with her back turned to me. I ran up and grabbed her shoulder to talk to her, she spun around and both of her eyes were missing. I screamed, and woke up.

It was a dream. It was so vivid, I couldn't shake the feeling that I had used again. I got up and started pacing my room, trying to figure out what I should do. I went and talked to my peers. They shared their first using dreams with me and that was when I learned my dream was likely only going to be the first of many. I had a really long haul ahead of me between my vein obsession, my daily urges to run away, and now these god damned dreams. Luckily, I didn't have to go on this roller coaster alone, because I was surrounded by people going through the exact same thing.

Twenty

Taking Flight

⬯⬯⬯

The deepest scars in life rest beneath the surface.
   Afraid of everything.
   Trying to get out.
Always suppressed.
Their release sets forth a metamorphosis
that is forever changing with the ebb and flow of hope.
The Butterfly takes flight, not knowing how far it can go, but it soars with the
refreshing knowledge that it was cared for by another living being.
   It flies high, knowing the beauty that lives in this world.
   It is a beauty that hides in every single being, that sometimes just needs to be
unchained.

The next 30 days in treatment were a whirlwind adventure. I balked at the stupid sugar and caffeine rule as I snuck around and gobbled up as much as I could get my hands on. I wasn't sure if it was because I wanted the sugar rush or if it was because they told me to not to. I didn't really put a lot of thought into it. It's like when someone says don't touch a button, you gotta touch the damn button and that was that. I had a lot of problems with my obsessions creeping in, they were referred to as triggers.

A trigger is something that reminds a person of their drug of choice and usually sparks a really bad craving. My obsessions were disgusting, every time I saw a vein popping out on someone's body, I stared at it and felt a little adrenaline rush. It was sick, I hated being that person and I finally opened up about it. Once everyone was on the same page they would confront it daily with banter and jokes about how everyone knew when they were talking to me all I was hearing was, "vein."

Another surprising trigger for me was red Kool Aid. I was preparing red Kool Aid and when I poured the packet into the pitcher of water it looked exactly like blood rushing into the syringe. It triggered me, hard, and set me on a bad tailspin. I had to make it a point to pour the powder into an empty pitcher, then fill it up with the water, in order to avoid the trigger. It is amazing how far a person can spiral down, so far that the simple process of making cherry Kool Aid was too much to handle.

Oh, and what was with this vein and blood obsession anyways? It's as if vampires were molded after people like me. Junkies who fucked themselves with the needle so hard that they had this weird craving for blood. I was ashamed, but the amazing thing about treatment was that everyone accepted me and told me their stories of shame to top mine. It was great to be around others who never treated me like I was less than them.

Part of the program was to work the first three steps, but the remaining steps were meant to be saved until after treatment. Step one: we admitted we were powerless and that our lives had become unmanageable. I had this step one business down, this was exactly how I got the bed here in the first place. So, I was really happy because it was like being very well prepared for a final exam, and I knew I was gonna nail it. What I didn't expect is that I was required to write my story, they called it a 3-5-page substance abuse history.

The writing was easy for me, as I had been an avid creative writer since I knew how to write. The part that I didn't expect was that I was required to read it to my peers, the other 27 people in treatment. I had already turned it in by that point and I pleaded with Beth, "You need to give that back to me."

"No, you need to leave it the way it is."

"Nobody needs to know what happened."

"It's not about how they feel about it, it's about what you need to do for your recovery." She smiled at me as if saying sorry not sorry.

Reading it to the group turned out to be my hardest day in treatment. My substance abuse history was longer than five pages. It was gory, it was brutally honest, it told the tale of the countless hours I spent locked away in bathrooms, the bloody spoons, the humiliating drawer, the everything including some stuff from my childhood that I didn't normally tell anyone about.

Twenty-One

Cinderella Watch

*R*oses are red.
  Violets as blue.
  I have never met a maiden as brutal as you.

One year for my birthday my mother gave me a Cinderella watch. I had coveted one of these watches for so long, I was ecstatic to receive this gift. It was a dream come true and it was unquestionably the coolest item I owned. It was in one of the colors I loved most: baby blue.

This was proof that in spite of all of our ups and downs, my stepmother definitely loved me, she obviously knew me very well and wanted me to be happy.

Who wants to focus on homework when they could sit at the kitchen table, stare at the sparkles on the face of their new stylish watch, listen to the sizzle of grease in a frying pan and enjoy the aroma of flour breaded pork chops that their step mom was cooking. I rubbed at the glass on the watch, examining every detail of Cinderella's dress.

I was concentrating so hard, she startled me when she came up and asked, "What time is it?" I jumped in my seat and looked up. She was standing there, coy grin on her face, one hand on her hip and the other holding a spatula.

Feeling ashamed for not paying more attention to my homework, I hung my head and guiltily replied, "Sorry."

I adjusted my stare back to my homework.

She smiled warmly and kindly forgave my disobedience.

School and following rules was a very important matter in our household. "I'm pleased you like it but I want you to tell me...what time is it?"

I felt really confused by her question. I stared at the numbers on the watch again and told her which numbers the little arrows were pointing at. "Its five-three," I said shyly.

It was her turn to look perplexed. She stared at me in confusion and asked me again, "What time is it?"

Again, I looked at the watch face, staring at the numbers. I presumed I had answered incorrectly the first time and hoping with all my might to answer the question correctly, I tried again. "Three-five?" I replied hesitantly.

She walked over to me and giggled while pointing at the hands on the watch. "Here's how it works. The little hand is the hour and the big hand tells you the minutes."

As realization dawned on me, I laughed and said, "Ohhhhh, that's how it works." I almost felt relief at having figured out how to tell time. We hadn't covered manual clocks in school yet, so no wonder I was bewildered.

She rubbed me on the shoulder in a very supportive manner "Sweetie, I wish I had known you didn't understand how to read the time when I gave you this watch," she stated sympathetically, "Now that I have explained how it works, tell me what time it is."

Feeling more confident, I replied, "It's five - three."

My answer was apparently incorrect because I could tell my stepmother was beginning to get exasperated and this heightened my anxiety. "No, June," she responded sharply, "It's five fifteen. Use your fives to count the minutes." She gestured at the watch and showed me how each number represented five minutes, "Five, ten, fifteen - now you count the rest."

I began counting all the little lines in between the numbers. "Okay. One, two, three, four, five..."

All of a sudden, she angrily grabbed the wrist the watch was on and started shaking it, "Why are you being so difficult!" she demanded furiously. "I know you know how to do this! You're too old not to know multiplication!"

In our household, deliberate laziness and disobedience required harsh punishment. My stepmother was absolutely convinced I was lying.

After a week or so of treacherous nights at the dining room table, going over and over multiplications, she was finally convinced I did not know how to multiply. This led to long lectures of how I should be ashamed of myself, that no eleven-year old child should be unable to do this and she knew I was smarter than that. She considered this a rebellious act of defiance, towards her.

It was such a simple task!! What was my problem? Didn't she think or realize that maybe it was the way she was teaching me? Or maybe that she put me under so much pressure, creating an overwhelming sense of anxiety, that my brain shut down and I couldn't even think, for fear of giving the wrong answer.

Come hell or high water, I was going to learn how to multiply immediately and spare our family the embarrassment. To top it all off, she warned me that she would begin showing me flash cards and if I didn't get the problem right, she would hit me in the face with a belt. I was doomed. Who could learn under these circumstances? The pressure of the looming threat made it impossible to succeed. Even the multiplication that I did know, came out wrong.

Flash cards are like surprise quizzes and with so much on the line, I froze with each card. She was careful to make sure I always knew that it was hurting her more than it hurt me and that it was impossible to teach me any other way. Tough love is what she called it and she made good on her promises with the belt.

This ordeal did not accomplish anything and it went on for weeks until she finally just gave up. This was the first major incident with her of that nature and it must have been around this time that I began wetting the bed every night.

This enraged her even more than the flash cards. She warned me that if I didn't stop she would tell all of my friends, and she did.

I still wet the bed.

She warned me that if I wanted to act like a dog, she would train me like a dog. She didn't want to, but I would be leaving her no choice.

I continued to wet the bed and she made good on those threats too by rubbing my nose in it.

Twenty-Two

Puppy Training

D ust particles glimmer in flight.
Sequins sparkle in the starry night.
Hope and magic glimmer bright as we get ready for the show tonight.
The show, the play called life, in which "The world is a stage and all the men and women are merely players" Shakespeare.

This begins a different chapter of our relationship and my abuse. The spankings I received were severe enough to leave welts and bruises all over my body, especially my legs. Before I begin the chapter of my life I refer to as Puppy Training, I would like to include a few other things. These incidents are separate but kind of meld together and appear, it seems, to happen simultaneously. As the time frame is the beginning and spans approximately the first year, one thought leads to another and another, reminding me of this or that, creating a mashed potato effect – they are all lumped together. It's important to me to recall these events together, as it is also the beginning of the end of my childhood.

One weekend before Christmas break, I was grounded. At this point, I cannot or choose not to remember, so basically, I am not sure why. My stepmother had gone Christmas shopping and while she was away, I went

156

out to the garage to listen to the stereo and dance. I was also visiting with friends, from inside the garage, with the big door open. I was having a great time, getting a groove on, practicing my moves when she came home sooner than I expected. I knew I shouldn't be out there, so I ran into the house. I guess I wasn't fast enough because she was hot on my tail and chasing me into my room. She proceeded to beat the tar out of me, with a belt, for a long time.

I didn't realize I was screaming so loud but I guess the whole neighborhood heard me because a little while later police officers showed up at the house. They were there to check on me as a concerned neighbor had called to report the screaming. I told them I was fine. Wouldn't good, concerned cops check out my story? I guess not with a stepmother hovering over me and repeating I was fine, describing how I was singing at the top of my lungs and of course, my caterwauling could definitely be misheard as screaming.

A few days later, we were sitting down to dinner when my stepmother informed me that my dad was "making" her let me off of grounding for Christmas break. I was overjoyed to hear this and called my girlfriend right after dinner. We planned to get together the next day.

We were hanging out, talking about school, our favorite movies, our crushes from the movies, what we hoped Santa would put under the tree and trying to guess what our parents would give us. Being girls and caught up in a world of fantasy, we decided to pretend we were going to a Christmas ball.

We pulled out bobby pins, hairspray, clips and bows to create updos with our hair, costume jewelry and some make-up her mom and passed along for this exact reason: a world of make believe.

Then, we went through her closet and pulled out some dresses we wanted to try on for the Prince Charming that would take us to the ball. As I was changing, my friend noticed my bare legs. Her eyes widened as she looked down and pointed at my leg. In a hushed voice, she asked me what happened. I glanced down and saw the whole side of my leg was black, blue and purple.

I explained I got in trouble for being outside while I was grounded. I recall at the time having no idea that what had happened to me was wrong because this type of thing was so normal at home. In fact, this was a lot less severe than some of the other things I had been through.

My friend had a very pained look on her face and shortly afterwards, she left the room to get us some snacks. A few moments later, her mother came in the room and was looking at my leg, a concerned look on her face. I could tell by the determined expression on her face this was not going to end well.

Before I could even process what was going on, the police showed up and my parents were called. Of course, my dad was away on one of his regular out of town trips and I was left with the evil stepmother. We were taken to the police station, they took pictures of the bruises all over my body, with extra photos of the ones on my legs. I was interviewed for an agonizingly long time, or at least what felt like eons, seeing as I was only a kid. I honestly cannot remember all of what I said, other than that my stepmother was exceptionally mean and very, very cruel.

Twenty-Three

A Normal Life

What is normal?

Is it the same for everyone?

Is it the pitch we are all given when we are kids?

At what phase in our lives do we wander out of what is considered normal, into the abnormal?

Is there a golden rule somewhere that defines normal, or is it just what we are force fed growing up, as in: finish school, get a career, get a job, buy a house, get married, have kids, and all of that? I suppose that Gay men and women can answer this question the most as they fight for the right to same sex marriage or to begin families of their own.

Normal, was defined for us all a long, long, time ago.

Every once in a while someone challenges that term and then real change can begin to happen. The only real thing that is certainly normal is "You will be given a body, take care of it because it's the only one you get."

The room was so quiet that you could hear a tiny pin drop. The counselors running the group gave us all frequent breaks, stating that it was too intense to hear it all in one session. At the very end, I had written a sentence that I rushed through as quickly as possible. Out of everything in there that I

159

shared, it was the primary sentence I wanted to erase, then I said it, as quickly as I could. "When I was 13 I was raped multiple times while hitchhiking."

I think I kind of expected the ceiling to fall down when I said it. I didn't feel like it was going to be ok to say it, it was like it made it too real again. It was something that I had spent a lot of years trying to forget about and it wasn't ok to speak it. "Do you want to talk about that?" a counselor said.

"No!" I kind of shouted at him while I stared at the floor. I was embarrassed, for some reason, I was just embarrassed. My face felt hot, I must have been red. I didn't look at anyone for a while the rest of that day, at least not in the face. I kept expecting something to happen because I said the magical words. It felt like walking out onto a stage, naked.

That is the best way to describe how it feels to share something, a secret, from the past that we swore we would never tell anyone about, ever. But I said it out loud and nothing happened. It didn't fit into the illusion of *normalcy* that *society*expected. I was *abnormal*, everything in my life was abnormal.

The bedwetting, the not being able to tell time, rapes, and other experiences in my life. Every single one of them played a part in turning me into the person I was on this day. I had never told anyone about any of that stuff and I was really surprised the sky didn't fall when I spoke it, out loud.

Then I moved on to step two: we came to believe that a power greater than ourselves can restore us to sanity. I sat with my counselor discussing the step and she asked me, "Who is your God?"

"Ummm, I don't know."

"Well, do you believe in God?"

"I definitely believe in something."

"Describe what you believe in."

"I don't really know how to describe it."

"When you think of God, what do you see?"

"I don't know, maybe a bright light?"

"When you do know, come and tell me. Because you can't finish step two until you do."

I was disappointed as I walked out of there. It seemed like I was going to fail step two and I couldn't let that happen. I was determined figure it out so I went out of my way to talk to people. I focused on their eyes, if I saw something special in their eyes I would stare into their eyes and try to figure out what I was seeing. I truly believed I could see the real person that way and if they were truly connected to a higher power, there would be a certain sparkle of happiness in there. When I found one of these people, I would interrogate them, asking, "What is your secret?"

"Secret to what?"

"God, you have found your higher power, I can see it in your eyes."

They would normally just laugh at me like I was weird and the most I could get from anyone is that they would just keep doing what was put in front of them and trust the outcome to their higher power.

Days went on and I accomplished nothing. Then one day, sitting in one of the boring educational video classes, I was nodding off like I always did, but I woke up hearing some golden words: "Where does God live?"

I perked up and paid attention to the Father Martin video. He was a priest with this entire series of 12 step videos. Sitting through one was kind of unbearably boring but what happened next was nothing short of mesmerizing to me. He said, "God's disciples asked Him where He wanted them to build His house, at the bottom of the ocean? And God said, 'no, they'll look there.' And God's disciples said, 'well how about at the top of a mountain?' God said, 'no, they'll think to look there too.'" Then Father Martin stopped, and giggled. "I want you to build my house inside of each and every one of them, they'll never think to look there."

I sprang up and ran to Beth's office. "I know where God is!"

She smiled at me. "Where?"

"He lives in my heart, and all around me." I got a little misty eyed as I said it, and Beth shed a tear with me.

"Good work, June."

I went back and watched the rest of the video, hanging on every word that was said. This was a pivotal moment for me as I sat and thought about all of the years I wandered through my life aimlessly trying to find something better. I felt so lost, so alone, so hopeless, I never knew that the answers to life's questions lived inside of me, I just had to stop numbing them with the drugs long enough to pay attention.

I found myself that day, in that moment. I found the inner beauty that was always there and that I just couldn't see. I am not a religious person, I am a spiritual person. I don't go to church, I have no religious upbringing, but there is a God, that lives inside of each and every one of us.

The beauty of the 12-step program is that we trust that doing the next right thing will always lead to the next right thing. Doing the wrong thing always leads to the next wrong thing. So, when we are tired of the bad situations we put ourselves in, we focus on the next right thing.

We don't always magically know what the next right thing is, sometimes we need to weigh our pros and cons to figure it out. But our instinct, the internal voice of right and wrong. That's where God lives and if we follow that inner voice to do the right thing, our lives will only soar by leaps and bounds.

I was a changed woman that day but I still had a lot of work to do. First, I had to clear up the warrant that was lingering for failing Drug Diversion. I showed up in court, was remanded into custody for a couple of hours, and then I was released. Why? Because I was doing the right thing and the next right thing happened. I was placed on the Addicted Offender Court Supervision program so I had a long legal haul ahead of me, but it was for my own good.

I started nearing my 45-day completion date and totally freaked out. The only place I had to go was Tabitha's. I didn't expect the treatment center to be able to help me with this so I kept my fears inside — that was the next wrong thing.

I started sneaking off to have sex with a male resident. One day we were supposed to meet and I had this sudden twinge of guilt that I was making a mistake. I had already snuck off with him a few times and we almost got caught. That was exactly how I could get myself kicked out of the program, which I really didn't want.

Sadly enough, at the exact time I was supposed to arrive at the rendezvous point, a female was viciously murdered. Her head had been cut off, in a rape and robbery. The front page of the newspaper had a photo of our meetup spot. It was a close up of the exact place I was supposed to be meeting him. Who knows what would have happened if I had been there. I felt terrible for the woman it happened to, and ironically enough the responding officer on scene was Deputy Corbin.

As I read the article all I could think of is how crazy it was that I was planning to be at that exact same spot at the exact same time, if I had been there it could have been me. Deputy Corbin would have been finding my dead body, after all of our interactions over the years, imagine how ironic that would have been? Or, imagine if they had killed her right in front of me but left me alive? Then Deputy Corbin would have found me at the scene of a murder. I couldn't imagine that would have ended well for me, in any way, shape or form. My inner voice told me not to go and for once I actually listened.

I went straight to Beth and told her. "I've been sabotaging myself because I feel like this whole program has been a waste of time, I'm going to get out of here and have a needle in my arm the first day." I broke down in tears. "I was going to go for a walk and a woman was raped and murdered in the exact place I was going!" I handed her the newspaper. "Do you think it was supposed to have been me?" I was panicking, breathing really heavily and shaking.

Beth moved to the chair next to me and put her arms around me. "Calm down and tell me what is going on."

"I don't have anywhere to go."

Beth looked at me long and hard. "Well, let's see if we can do something about that."

"How? I have no money. I've never not been homeless."

"What do the 12-steps tell us to do, June?"

"Do the footwork and leave the results up to God."

"Just remember that and stay positive."

Well, the rest that happened was yet another miracle. I reported to AOP court and told the judge what was going on, he pulled some strings and got me a 15-day extension, so we officially had two weeks to find a place for me to go.

Then Beth pulled some strings and I suddenly had a two-bedroom apartment all to myself. I told the people who managed it that I had no money and they didn't care. This was a sober living apartment complex for Native Americans but after my counselor had told them my story they just wanted to help me succeed. They actually let me move in with no money at all, they turned on the electricity for me and told me that when I had income, they would base my rent on the income. I would never be asked to leave unless I broke the obvious golden rule: no drug use.

So, miraculously enough, my first prayer in my entire life hit me like a tornado of miracles. I went from being a hopeless, disgusting, rock bottom junkie, who prayed for death. To having my entire life turned upside down in the most amazing way by being shoved into treatment. My first days there I nearly died, but I survived. I found God and ultimately found myself along the way. I suddenly wasn't homeless anymore and I went from a hopeless existence to a life that was brimming with possibilities, all in a matter of 60-days. My new apartment was only two blocks from the truest home I have ever had the honor of living in. Which was great because I needed all of the support I could get.

I gave everyone a hug and headed to my new apartment. The walk was interesting, as I knew that I was walking to the start of my brand-new life, and at the age of 25 I still had time to do a lot of the things that being a junkie had stolen from me. I was proud of who I was in this moment, helped so graciously by the kindness of strangers.

I was the butterfly.

Who knows?

Maybe I had one coming to me for helping that butterfly such a long time ago. It was really just a butterfly with a broken wing, but the kindness of a stranger showed that butterfly the beauty that lives in this world.

The beauty is love, care, and selflessness – that is the beauty that repaired his wing and helped him to fly again.

This beauty has not been lost in the world, it still exists, in a place of magic that lives inside of each and every one of us.

Be still and listen to your inner voice, do you hear it?

I could never hear my inner voice until I had a spiritual awakening, the burning bush, the sudden introduction to, me. Up until I realized exactly who I was, I had been walking around a stranger in my own mind.

I mean yeah, I recognized who I saw in the mirror but that's because I conditioned myself to recognize her. Who I really was, but couldn't ever see, was all of my experiences.

When I set out to party, thinking it was all about having a good time, I never realized what I was really doing was finding the only comfort I could because I had no idea who I was and no idea where to go or what to do with my life.

Walking out of treatment a new woman was exciting, but I was walking into my first apartment, my first real experience as an adult with bills I would have to pay, a home I would have to furnish.

How would I do any of that stuff?

One day at a time I suppose.

Twenty-Four

Aftercare

～⚬⚬⚬～

*L*ife.
A dance with mirrors.
An empty space of inadequacy that we don't even realize we're trying to sell.

Being in my first place was exciting but scary at the same time. I didn't have any furniture, the only belongings I had were at my old using pad – the thought of walking back in there was kind of scary.

Luckily for me, a higher power was definitely looking out for me. Everything I needed pretty much appeared as if it were magic. Within a week I had a couch, an old rabbit ear TV, and a few dishes - but I made a big mistake.

While I was in treatment I had started sneaking off with a guy, the guy I was supposed to meet the day of the murder on the river trail. He was 25 years older than me and had just served 20 years in Prison. I think what had attracted me to him was his strength and persona of responsibility. I mean, he seemed to have his shit together and seemed very self-confident.

I was young, immature and very insecure. My time seeing him in treatment was just so that I could focus on someone else and not feel so alone. I was using him which I didn't see as a bad thing because he was obviously using me too – we were using each other for sex.

I attempted to break it off with him as I left treatment, because I was never intending on it being a long relationship, but he broke down crying when I tried to. I wasn't expecting this guy, a hardened Parolee, covered in tattoos, same age as my father, to break down crying and begging me to keep seeing him.

I had been cold when breaking off relationships before, but this time I was fresh out of recovery and very vulnerable. I caved and shortly afterwards he moved in with me. Not really sure why I did that but I definitely felt insecure on my own and moving him in brought me a sense of security.

The relationship was ok at first but there were some hiccups and moments where he became verbally abusive. We attended counseling sessions pretty early on to try and work things out.

He was working full time and paying all of the bills while I enrolled in college to pursue my degree as a residential counselor.

So, when things got ugly between us, I was always trying to find a way to fix it because leaving didn't seem like it was possible. We became on site managers of an apartment complex and were engaged to be married.

I had invited my dad to the wedding but he said that it was on the weekend of his annual golfing trip with Grandpa, so he was sorry but he couldn't make this one, and he would be sure to "Catch the next one" I was pissed when he said that but a time came when I eventually got the joke.

A few days before our wedding, my fiancé and I went to pick up these decorations and I accidentally directed him to turn into the wrong parking lot. He pulled over the truck, grabbed me by both arms, and started viciously shaking me, screaming at me about how stupid I was.

He calmed down and drove us home without hitting me but he had squeezed my arms so hard they were swelling. On the day of our wedding I walked down the aisle with handprint bruises. I questioned the marriage, I did, but fear of losing my lifeline ushered me down that aisle anyways.

Our marriage was incident free for a short while until one morning when I was driving him to work. I had a 1977 Chevy Camaro, which will always be my favorite car. It was a great car but on cold mornings it needed a special touch, so as not to flood the carburetor.

On this particular morning, I made the mistake of stepping on the gas when I fired it up and it did what it would do, it flooded the carburetor. He became furious with me. Screaming at me, at the top of his lungs, so loud that every single vein on his face was bulging.

"YOU STUPID BITCH!!" he shouted.

I ignored him as I drove.

"YOU KNOW I HAVE TO BE AT WORK AND YOU'RE MAKING ME LATE!!" he continued shouting.

As loud as he was, my own thoughts became loud enough that his screams began to drift away as I asked myself: *Why am I living this way? Did I really come this far with my life, with my recovery, just to be screamed at this way? And if our lives are predetermined by a higher power, the driving force of destiny, if everything is exactly the way it is supposed to be at this moment and nothing happens in God's world by mistake, then it's God that that put me in this situation, right? And why? Is there some sort of lesson I'm supposed to learn here?*

His belligerent screaming went on, I shut it back out to return to my own private confrontation.

I asked, within myself, "God, I understand that nothing happens in my life by mistake. I understand that in order to have any serenity in my life I need to accept that everything in my life, including the people in it, are exactly the way they are supposed to be at this time. The only thing I have any control over is my perception, my reaction. So please help me understand WHY THIS? Why do I have to be subjected to this abuse? What is the lesson plan here?"

I had been praying pretty consistently since my days in treatment and on this day I actually *heard* an answer, "You don't" said a very clear voice from within.

"Oh" I said as this bright light began to emanate from within - effectually liberating me from the self made prison of an abusive and loveless marriage of opportunity. Being exactly where we are supposed to be in this moment, does not mean we have to live in an unhappy situation.

Some situations in our lives are just a bridge that help us get to where we need to go, the challenge is realizing it is a bridge so that we can cross it to get to our better path and by the time I dropped him off at work I was filled with excitement about my future. A life without him in it looked like a happy one indeed.

I headed off to work myself, I was an assistant Shotokan Karate Sensei at the community college. What had started as a general education elective had blossomed into something that I had really poured myself into. Something about my time in training just helped me feel centered.

There was also this big social world in Karate, Boxing, MMA and I had begun training in other Dojo's on my off days from Shotokan so I spent five days a week in Dojo's. After doing that for some time my Sensei recommended that the college hire me for the Karate summer camp, which meant eight solid hours per day training. That day I was teaching front kicks which meant eight solid hours of front kicks, back and forth, across the studio.

Prior to leaving the house that morning, I had started dinner in the crock pot and set the table which was also something I did every day - for him. When I got home, I walked in and found him sitting at the table - which was pretty standard. I assumed he would be in a better mood, considering all of the hours that had passed since the Carburetor issue of the morning.

He quietly looked at me, holding up a fork.

I looked at the fork, confused.

"Why do you insist on giving me the forks that I don't like!" he growled.

"What are you talking about?" I chuckled.

"You know I hate this fork" he growled.

"You're fucking kidding me right?" I said to him - laughing.

He glared.

"I have no idea what your problem is, if you really have an issue with the fork just get yourself a new one" I said to him.

"I HATE LITTLE FORKS! I HAVE TOLD YOU OVER AND OVER AGAIN YOU FUCKING IDIOT!!!!" he shouted as he charged towards me.

I was still standing at the front door as he gained ground. He threw the fork and reached for my throat.

A moment later he was on the floor, rolled up in a fetal position and sobbing like a child. It was all so sudden I wasn't sure exactly what happened until he looked at me, with *the look*.

About a year before this incident, in our first apartment, he had taken a job as a roofer. One night when he came home he started having these horrible leg cramps that he was moaning and crying about "Hot baths always help me with cramps" I said to him as I ran a bath.

He crawled into the bathroom, crying and moaning in pain.

I fought it back as much as I could but then it came. It was like a dam broke or something, as everything in me knew it was wrong but it was just too powerful to fight, I laughed. Then as he looked at me I could see it all over his face, he had the expression of a wounded animal being prodded at and poked by a sadistic antagonist.

Sadly, the look on his face only made me laugh more. I knew it was wrong but that just made it even funnier - I could not stop laughing. It was not lost on me that the reason I felt so heartless in the presence of his suffering was because of how horribly he treated me.

On this day, in this moment, he looked at me that way again and I realized my front kick had flowed so naturally I took him down without even realizing I was doing it. I did not want to deal with the aftermath of his rage once the pain of being kicked so hard in the nuts had passed.

I had already had a moment of clarity earlier that day, that had adjusted my sails "so to speak" so it was now just a matter of going. I had wanted to make arrangements for where I was going, before actually going, but in this moment. It was just time.

I think that in a multitude of ways I had been this mans captive for a long time. I believe that on an emotional level, I rolled with this one out of fear of being on my own. I was afraid I would not be able to keep a roof over my head. I was afraid I wasn't responsible enough to pay my bills. I was afraid so I sought a relationship with someone who knew how to do all of that and could tell me what to do.

Over time I became dependent on that when he took over all of those responsibilities and we both stepped into the roles that I had cast us in. He was the responsible one, I was the weak stupid one not responsible enough to do anything. Not even smart enough to give the guy the fork he preferred when I set his table for him.

He was performing the role I had cast him in, and I was performing the role I had cast myself in. It was the bridge that helped me realize there was a lot more to me than I had ever given myself credit for. It's funny how much clearer everything gets when we look back, hindsight being in 3D.

Imagine how much easier life would be if we could be more aware of the self image we have strapped ourselves with? Life is a dance with mirrors, in each mirror we're all looking for someone to fill an empty space of inadequacy that we don't even realize we're trying to sell. Every single one of us is looking for that soul to squeeze but we will never achieve the fulfillment we are looking for when we search outside of ourselves.

Twenty-Five

New Beginnings

F aith without works is dead.
  Faith without works is dead.
  Faith without works is dead.

At one point in my life I wasn't entirely sure what *faith without works is dead* meant because I had to take a leap of faith in order to find out. It goes back to this joke I heard when I was younger about the capsized boat in the middle of the ocean.

There were twelve people on a boat that sank in the middle of the ocean, one of them was a Pastor. He prayed for God's help and it didn't take long for a rescue boat to come along, just as he knew it would, but sadly they didn't have room for everyone.

The Pastor was asked to climb aboard, but he recoiled from the outstretched hand, "No, take the others, I trust that God will protect me" he said.

"Are you sure?" the rescuer replied.

"Oh yes son, I have faith" the Pastor responded.

A little while later a helicopter came, just as the Pastor knew it would, and once again there was not enough space for everyone that needed rescuing.

The Pastor insisted they take everyone else, while he wait for the next rescue. He drowned.

When he got to heaven he asked, "God, why did you help me? I acted in faith but you let me drowned."

"I sent two boats and a helicopter" God answered.

Moral of the story, it's one thing to have faith, it's another to act on it and it's also another thing to do the footwork. We can pray all day long but taking a true leap of faith is trusting a stairwell that we cannot see, doing the footwork that will help us get to where we are trying to go, and accepting the help that is presented to us.

The day I heard the soft voice tell me I didn't have to be there I knew that all I had to do is leave and everything I needed would be provided somehow. So I left, and called a friend who immediately let me come to stay with her. That night, as I was going to bed, I prayed.

"God, I am scared. I just left and I have nowhere to live, I have no job, I have no money, and I could really use your help. I took a leap of faith and I pray you'll help me see what to do next. Thank you."

The next day.

Literally the very next day.

I was hired as an on-site manager for an apartment complex, by the same company I had been working for with my husband. They also advised they still owed me money from a unit I had painted for them, and had a check waiting for me.

Within the next couple of days, I also landed three more part-time jobs, one of them was as a Counselor at a DUI school, another as a housekeeper, and a work from home job for a psychic network. I suppose I was overcompensating getting so many part time jobs, but it was clear that my leap of faith was exactly what I needed to do.

My abusive husband attempted to reconcile but I literally would no longer spare another ounce of my energy listening to him or talking to him. I filled out all of the divorce paperwork myself, while I was working at the DUI school. There were educational classes every day in which the students watch videos, so I sat in the back of the classroom and muddled my way through it, although I had never been through a divorce before.

It was an end to that chapter of my life, and at that point I had 3 ½ years clean. Around that time I had a sudden recollection of a guy named Justin that I hadn't seen since before I went into recovery

The last time I had seen him, we were both inmates in the county jail, I was in the process of being released when I saw him come out of the medical wing to hop on an elevator back to his pod.

"I got sentenced to 6 years" he said.

"Ah shit, that sucks" I said to him as he disappeared into the elevator. I hadn't really thought about him since.

The way he used to look at me, I had a hunch that he may have found me attractive, I definitely found him attractive but he was the boyfriend of a good friend of mine so that was that. On this day when I thought of him, I kind of wondered what it would have been like if circumstances had been different.

A few days later I went to my Narcotics Anonymous meeting home group. Home group is a phrase to describe the meeting that you never miss, it's a core support group that you always attend no matter what.

I was sitting at the table when I felt a tap on my shoulder, and as I stared at him I wasn't sure at first who I was looking at but it looked at lot like him.

"Remember me?" he laughed.

"Oh shit, I was just thinking about you the other day!" I said as I got up and hugged him.

We didn't have any more time to talk, because the meeting was starting but we found each other outside during the 15-minute break.

"I just got out of Prison" he said.

"Wow, it's awesome to see you here" I said.

"So you're clean now?" he asked.

"Yep, got 3 ½ years" I said.

"Sweet!" he said.

"Yeah, I work at a DUI school and I was in college but I'm taking a break right now" I told him.

"I'm in a half-way house till I get back on my feet, but I just got a job so I'm saving up for my own place" he said. Then he handed me a piece of paper with his number on it "Let's hang out sometime" he said.

I wrote my number down and gave it to him "Definitely" I said "I just moved into my new place and I'm getting the phone set up soon" I told him.

"Alright well let me know if you need any help" he said as he went back into the meeting.

I was blown away by running into him just after thinking about him, and even more surprised when a couple of weeks later I started coming home from my multiple jobs to find messages on my answering machine from him, "Hi, it's Justin, just calling to see how you're doing."

Then the next day, another message from him. I kept missing him due to all of the jobs I was juggling but finally we connected, and he brought me some stuff for my new place. Eventually we went on a date, eventually we were a couple, and eventually we were having a baby.

Everything was pretty sweet; we were on the same wave link somehow. Anything I thought of he seemed to be thinking too as if we were somehow mirroring each other. On Christmas I decided to surprise him with a leather jacket, much to my dismay he also surprised me with a leather jacket.

It seemed to be a perfect match.

A Real World Fairy Tale

⚬⚬⚬

*A*t this point I had close to five years clean, was very pregnant with my only child and everything in my life was perfect. I took Justin home to meet my parents for Christmas. My dad and my stepmother were very excited about the new baby and so proud of what I was doing with my life. They both cracked jokes about the previous husband being so old and of course my dad pointed out that he knew it would be short lived – hence his comment about *catching the next one* which wasn't meant as any kind of a joke.

By the last day of the visit my mother sat me down to have a talk with me. It felt awkward because I had not had a one on one talk with her since I was a little kid, and even then we weren't talkers – we were fighters. The hand-to-hand combat, knockdown, drag out, roll around the living room kind of talkers so I guess it was all about the body language ya know?

Our last one on one *conversation* that I could remember was way back when I was thirteen, she slapped me for mouthing off, I hit her back. It was the first time I had ever hit her back and fist-a cuffs it was!

She was enraged that I had the nerve to hit her back, I mean the whole reason she slapped me was for mouthing off. We rolled around, landing on the coffee table, then to the floor, and somehow up onto the couch.

Then I ran away and I ended up in juvenile hall when I got caught shoplifting cigarettes. I sat in Juvenile Hall waiting to be picked up, but my dad was out of town on a business trip and mom had apparently decided to let me rot there. After some time, I was declared an "Unwanted Child" by the Judge, due to the fact that my parents were aware that they had to pick me up and chose not to.

It was awkward, standing in the courtroom among all of those people, hearing the judge announce me as an "Unwanted Child" as he officially declared me a Ward of the court. I was remanded into court custody until my eighteenth birthday, it felt like a pretty harsh punishment for the fight.

My dad, he was out of town on business when all of this went down. "I tried to talk to the judge to get them to let me take you home, but it was too late" he said as he cried in the visiting room.

Then the visit was over and I headed back to my cell. Up until that moment, I had always thought that as soon as my Dad came home, he'd put a stop to all of this. He'd be enraged with my stepmother for leaving me to rot in there. He'd be enraged with the judge; he'd move mountains and bring me home from this place.

As the large, heavy metal door slammed shut it echoed through my thoughts. Haunting every fiber of my being like a good, scary Stephen King novel. A ward of the court until my 18th birthday. The remainder of my teenage years locked away as a prisoner.

After all of the fighting with my stepmother, I finally stood up to her. I won. Or at least I thought I won, but in the end she definitely got the last word. I wondered if hitting her back that day was worth it, and the rebellious side of me said "Fuck yeah it was" as I sat on my bunk and cried.

Her and I had not had a lot of one on one meet ups since then, but throughout my years in court custody I always returned home for Christmas and we got along very well. Probably because we both knew the visit would be short and as soon as the Holiday was over, I'd be heading back to the group home.

When I turned 18, she allowed me to return home. We got along ok but in a lot of ways it seemed we kept our distance from each other. Neither one of us wanted to revisit the past and a time came when she advised I was making it difficult for her to get along with my dad.

My dad got involved to the extent of giving me a deadline to sign up for Boot Camp. He felt strongly that the Army was the best choice for me and if I didn't go I'd be out on my ass. I thought what he was doing was very unfair. I had literally just spent my teenage years in court custody. I realized I was getting too old to keep living at home but I had a full time job and was trying to find my footing.

I'd like to say I had a nice savings account, but the truth is, I had a nice savings built up from the jobs I had in the group home. Once I was cut loose, I had access to the account, and I splurged. The most expensive purchase was a beautiful music box that I bought for my stepmother for Christmas.

It cost me half of my savings and it was the most expensive thing I had ever bought for anyone; it was made of 24 carat gold. It was not lost on me that I was spending the most on her. Even though we fought a lot, I always sought her love and approval. It was my dwindling savings, and my late nights out with my friends that led to my dad kicking me out.

From there, I stayed with friends as much as I could, but a time came when I was walking the streets all night with nowhere to go. I frequently broke into my dad's garage late at night to steal food from the freezer and sleep on a couch he had in there. I also frequently called him begging for money for food and after giving me some trouble he'd meet me somewhere or wire the money to me but I could not return home.

I always felt it was my stepmother that straddled me with homelessness. I knew that if she had not given my dad such a hard time about me, the situation would have been different.

I also felt hurt that I wasn't his first choice. There was some jealousy on my part that he always seemed to choose her over me, even when it meant my homelessness. All that being said, I was also a self-loather of biblical proportions. In many ways, I did not, nor had I ever, felt good enough for anything at all. I felt like all I really did in life was occupy space.

So here we are, I returned home to visit for Christmas. I was finally doing more than occupying space, I was a counselor, I was enrolled in school, I had a new love in my life and was finally becoming a mother.

Bringing life into the world is an amazing, miraculous gift of being a woman. It was really the first time in my life that I truly felt connected to the essence of what it means to be a woman, beyond being an object for men to take advantage of.

My stepmother, one of the most beautiful women I have ever known in my entire life, asked me to join her out front. We sat down across from each other at this quaint little round glass patio table with two cute little matching chairs.

"I wanted to let you know that I am dying, the doctors have given me six months" she said.

I froze. I didn't know what to say.

"You've probably been waiting to hear this your whole life, considering we didn't have a very good relationship" she said, looking down at the glass patio table.

I'm not sure what kind of facial expression I had, but I'm sure it wasn't appropriate because I was in absolute shock. Never had I ever had anyone drop a bomb like this on me, especially not a parent. Yeah, she was my stepmother, but she was truly the only mother I had ever known "No, I am really sad to hear this, isn't there anything they can do?" I asked.

"The doctor said they could normally remove the part of the lung that has the cancer, but my heart isn't strong enough to go through the surgery" she said.

Then she pulled something out of her pocket, it was an enormous Gold ring, she handed it to me, "I want you to have this. I am giving all of the kids something personal and this is for you."

"Wow" I said as I accepted her gift.

"And I want to apologize. I do believe in the afterlife and I feel I need to clean up some wrong doings before I go, you're one of the biggest apologies I feel I owe."

"I am sorry too" I said through the tears.

"Well, I'm going to admit I was always a little jealous, I think that's what the problem was. I was jealous of your dad's attention" she said.

I nodded.

"I think you were a little jealous too" she said with a grin.

"Yes, I think so too" I said to her although I didn't know if I meant it.

So, we sat there and forgave each other.

Or least that's what the spoken words were.

But I saw something in her eyes, it was a glimmer of an accusation. It was the glimmer she would get in her eyes when she woke me up at 3am to do the dishes, then she would pour coffee over the dishes that I had just washed so that I would have to wash them again.

It was the glimmer I saw in her eyes every time she would say something mean or say something that would leave me feeling embarrassed. The glimmer of my competitor. The one who my dad always sided with.

The rage of competition flared within me from a very deep and dark place that I didn't really understand. It was void of common sense, absent of rational thought, it was what Freud would call my "Id" reaction. It was very immature, unadulterated, almost as if an act of instinct.

Suddenly it was a race against time to win this thing, and I wasn't sure how. Then I realized, I was going to have to sacrifice my recovery and be the person I used to be, that was the only way to gain the upper hand and that was when this little voice in the back of my head, I suppose it was my inner junkie, as clear as a bell said "It's time to use again."

I would NOT let her win.

Twenty-Seven

Relapse

*R*arely have we seen a person fail who has thoroughly followed our path. Those who do not recover are people who cannot or will not completely give themselves to this simple program, usually men and women who are constitutionally incapable of being honest with themselves (How It Works - Big Book of Alcoholics Anonymous).

Many people wonder if relapse has to be a part of recovery. I had only been in a treatment center one time. I had only taken interest in recovery, one time, yet I had five years of clean time under my belt without a single relapse. As a DUI school counselor I highlighted this topic quite a bit along with the Disease Concept and Medical Aspects of addiction.

The Disease Concept theorizes that addiction to mood-and mind-altering substances needs to be treated as a disease. Medical Aspects cover a lot of areas but also the theory that addiction is hereditary. What that means is, if Grandpa was an alcoholic, odds are, others in the family also have the hereditary risk factor of becoming an alcoholic.

Alcoholism is addiction to alcohol.

Disease Concept theorizes that, once a person becomes addicted, that addiction can only be arrested by removing all mood/mind altering substances.

That basically means if Grandpa gave up the booze for pills, he would likely abuse the pills the same way he abused the booze - or the pills would simply lead him back to the booze because the booze is Grandpa's drug of choice.

Addiction is a beast sleeping within, even when it's not being fed by substances, it's always there, always waiting to be fed, always waiting to be woken up. Once it has been woken up, it can be put back to sleep through total abstinence but an addict cannot expect to keep it asleep if they continue to tempt it with more substances. When they do that they are simply trading one addiction for another and in some cases it leads to stronger cravings for the addicts drug of choice.

That was the golden rule I was taught in treatment and my addiction had been so miserable that when they told me that, it was really all it took to keep me from tempting fate. All I knew was, I didn't want to trade my new life for the old one, and if all I had to do was not use anything at all - that's what I was willing to do.

Keeping in mind that my situation had been utter hell. I was cutting myself in bathtubs to keep from getting caught by police that weren't even searching for me. I was homeless for so long. I had spent countless hours poking tens of thousands of holes into myself, surrounded by tens of thousands of little drops of blood from pulling out the syringe to hunt for a new vein.

I had literally stepped out of the gates of hell into heaven - so what I did was *I completely gave myself to the simple program* and had not experienced any relapse because I had had no desire to tempt fate. I was even taught to be sparing with harmless things like Aspirin and Ibuprofen - they said to be careful with all forms of drugs so I was. I frequently covered that with my clients at DUI school because many of them were still using substances in spite of their DUI's.

"Well have you tried having a drink or smoking pot since you kicked the needle?" a client said.

"No" I answered.

"Well then how do you know that it would lead you back to shooting up?" he asked.

"I don't have any proof" I said.

"Well then try it, it's the only way to find out" he said.

"I have weighed out the pros and cons of my old life vs the life that I have now and have decided it's not worth the risk" I said.

These words floated through my mind as my super-ego battled with the id inside of me. For the first time in my recovery I was questioning everything I had been taught and beginning to consider what my clients were telling me. It was clear that I was looking for rationalizations and validations to help me in my pursuit to win the race against my dying stepmother. The id is everyone's set of uncoordinated instinctual desires.

The super-ego plays the critical and moralizing role. The ego is the organized, realistic agent that mediates between the instinctual desires of the id and the super-ego (according to Sigmund Freud). The id in me led to the instinctual urge to use again before she died, it was the final battle to be the focal point of dads attention.

The super-ego was warning me against it, and the ego was basically threatened by the idea of losing everything I had built while the voices of my clients in the DUI school echoed in the back of my mind, helping me rationalize the fact that I might be able to control it *this time*.

One thing I would not do is use while pregnant, so this was going to be a well thought out plan to be implemented after my baby was born, crossing fingers my mother would hold on long enough because I was still four months away from my due date and I had to figure out how to talk Justin into relapsing with me.

I made up my mind to devise a plan that would allow us both to use again and get away with it. His parole was short so he was about to be in the clear from that aspect so all I had to do is keep us from falling off of the edge into addiction. I felt that with all of my experience as a counselor it would be easy.

So I continued to go about my life, continued working as a counselor, while secretly plotting my relapse in the back of my mind. I didn't tell anyone about it, because I knew they would try to talk me out of it and I didn't want to lose my job. What if I changed my mind somewhere along the way? I don't think it would be fair to lose my career over a fantasy of relapse.

I was attending all of my usual 12 step meetings and had a momentary lapse of insanity. I shared my relapse plans out loud. By the end of the meeting I was determined to save myself from myself, and I walked away with a plan. The next day I began having abdominal pains so I went to the hospital to get checked out.

They ran a bunch of tests and sent me home. Before I reached the house they called and asked me to come back "The Doctor that came on at shift change reviewed your file and feels that you need to come back to the hospital" the Nurse said.

"Is everything ok?" I asked.

"Yes, it's just for observation" she said.

"Oh, ok" I said.

"If you want you can bring some DVD's with you, it'll keep you occupied, then you can just spend the night and we'll send you home tomorrow" she said.

"Ok, great" I told her.

Justin and I rented a couple of movies and headed back to the hospital.

"What's happened was, you had a very small contraction and when that happened the babies heartbeat seemed like it might have been effected. It was very subtle so it's probably nothing to worry about but it's best to monitor for 24 hours so we can see if it is something to worry about" the Doctor said.

"Oh, ok, well thank you for spotting that and checking it out" I said.

Everything was fine all night and the next day the new shift doctor cut me loose. As the Nurse was removing all of the sensors the sonogram results from earlier that morning came in. She stared at them with concern, then did a final check on the babies heartbeat and his heartbeat was gone.

She got out additional equipment but still, the babies heartbeat wasn't there.

She hit a code blue and I had dozens of medical staff rushing around me, plus they called back the Doctor who had cut me loose. He had already headed to his car to go golfing and the Nurse advised me "You're not going home, you're having this baby" she stepped over with my sonogram pictures and showed me.

The umbilical cord was prolapsed, wrapped around his neck and head. Every time there was a contraction, the cord was choking him. I had had a recent sonogram, so whatever happened with the umbilical cord was fairly recent and may have had something to do with the baby rolling around in there.

"I didn't want to do this today, you're two months early, but we're concerned about the safety of the baby, so lets get in there and see what we're dealing with" the Doctor said as a fleet of Nurses rolled me down the hallways.

It was a very crash course delivery of my first baby and Justin held my hand through it all. I found the epidural to be wonderful but I also felt really nauseated knowing my stomach was completely opened up, of course Justin didn't help with that as he was giving me a blow by blow report of what my insides looked like.

Throughout the process my son did not have a heartbeat that they could find so the experience was very terrifying, none of us knew if he was going to survive. I felt the biggest sense of relief the moment I heard him cry. It took a little work on the Doctors part to make that happen, but once it did they let me hold my slimy miracle baby for about 30 seconds before they whisked him away to put him on life support. Then they whisked me away to my own hospital room on my own adult form of life support called a morphine drip.

My son was very premature so they needed to keep him sedated and on a ventilator in the NICU until they knew his lungs were strong enough to breath on his own. Due to the circumstances, they advised I would not be able to see him unless I could go there to see him and even then I would not be able to hold him until he was off of the ventilator.

The c-section was on the day before Mother's Day. I had no idea it was Mother's Day until the next day, when the NICU Nurses brought me a hand made Mother's Day card that included polaroid pictures of my son on all of the life support stuff. It was really awesome to see him and know that he was stable but there was something about it all that broke my heart too.

I am pretty sure this is when the depression started to creep in. I wasn't able to see my son until I was able to walk, but due to having Gestational Diabetes I had swelled up during my pregnancy to a little heavier than 200 pounds. Now with all of the staples in my stomach, attempting to stand was excruciating. On top of that, they had me on both Percocet and Morphine so I was lit and it added to the difficulty without removing the pain.

One night when they woke me at 3am for my Percocet I declined the pill, in hopes that I could get up and visit my son. I finally did manage to stand up. Blood gushed out of me onto the floor as my stomach lit up like someone had poured kerosene on it and set it on fire.

It was a painful experience, but I did manage to get to him. He was so beautiful. They had him in a medically induced coma, due to the ventilator, but I got to touch his hand and it was the softest thing I have ever felt in my life.

It gave me a new motivation that can't really be put into words. Over the next several days they woke him up and wanted me to try breast feeding him. I had very, very, large breasts so it was challenging to breast feed because as the Nurse described I needed to be careful not to smother him. He was having trouble latching on and at one point he looked up at me and I could see in his eyes he was bewildered about this stranger and the booby in his face.

I was suffering from Perinatal Depression, which is really not a strong enough phrase to describe what I was going through. I guess I had the *poor me's.* My first son and I couldn't even do anything right.

Plus, in the NICU there was another baby right next to him, completely blue, on his stomach and on some type of machine that shook him constantly.

"His lungs didn't fully develop so we have to keep him shaking to keep the oxygen flowing" the nurse said.

"Oh my god, that's so sad" I said.

"What's worse is, the whole thing could have been avoided with a sonogram, but the mom was on Medi-Cal and they aren't covering routine sonograms anymore" the nurse said, shaking her head in disgust.

"It is disgusting, the way they treat people on medi-cal, it's like just because they don't have money, they don't think they deserve proper medical care" I said to her.

"Oh honey, what's even worse is there's a hospital in Sacramento that can treat this baby, but he needs to be air lifted and Medi-Cal won't pay for that either" she said as she walked away.

I was finally sent home to recover but my son had to stay in the NICU. I visited him every day and watched this poor little baby suffer until a day came when he was gone. According to the Nurses, the helicopter was finally approved but it was too late.

My son was improving but had developed Jaundice. He had gained the nickname in the NICU of the California kid because of his super tan skin and the sunglasses they had on him to treat the Jaundice. Plus he was covered in beautiful blonde hair. He was so special, but I felt I struggled to have the bond I always expected us to have, which is probably because of how we were kept apart during his first weeks of life.

For the first time since having my spiritual awakening I became angry with God. I was angry about the world that we live in and began to accuse God of it being his fault – I decided I didn't want any part of the lie of a beautiful world where good things happen if this is the kind of stuff I'm going to have to go through.

It was a tantrum and I knew it as I started abusing the Percocet they sent me home with. It was when Justin caught me hiding the Percocet that I finally "pitched" the relapse plan to him. He immediately refused, he was so happy to be a new father and didn't want to do anything to put that at risk. Unfortunately, the beast was already very much reawakened within me and I kept chipping away at him.

I had a very unfair advantage, I was a master manipulator that had been plotting our demise for quite some time. I had all of the scenarios mapped out long before the birth of our son, I was just waiting to strike while the iron was hot. It was only a matter of time until he gave in.

Cogito Ergo Sum

I am destined for greatness.

I am destined for failure.

I am born of the pain dealt to me by others.

I am born of the pain dealt to me by my own hand.

I am a product of my own prison.

I am everything and nothing that burns within the fires deep down inside of these emotional walls.

I am the flame that draws the kindred spirits near from far and wide, to help ensure the destruction is pure, complete and final.

I am the destruction of my dark passenger.

I am the destruction of my own light.

I am the keeper of the kindred spirits that enter my life to attack both.

I am the only one with the choice to tame the fires because they are driven by my own thoughts, energy and intent.

I think, therefore I am.

Cogito ergo sum.

We drove down to show the baby to my parents. My mother was bedridden in my old room. She had managed to defy the six months the doctors had given her and said it came from reading "The Doctor Within." She held my baby for a long time, and it was beautiful. We showed her the VHS tapes of his nursery and she was cringing at how long my nails were, as it kept looking like I was gonna scratch him. I did not realize how long they were either till I saw it on video.

On the drive home I kept chipping away at Justin to use again.

"I wouldn't even know where to get any if I wanted to use again" he said, annoyed.

"Why don't you try asking around at work?" I suggested.

He did try and it didn't take long before the old Meth crowd began gravitating towards us. It is interesting how that works. It's like a gravitational pull in the universe, put out the energy long enough, focus on it and it's as if a gravitational pull draws the people into your life that match what you are feeling, seeking, focusing on.

We ended up running into our old dealer who we hadn't seen in years, then at her house I ran into some of my clients from DUI school. I was on a maternity leave, so it was pretty awkward to be hanging out with them.

At first, we had trouble finding syringes and attempted to use syringes that were made for horses. It wouldn't work in my veins because they were too small for the needle, but it wasn't long until I found a supplier of the type of needles I needed.

Next we met a new lady who happened to have pounds of Methamphetamine she was trying to sell, so she would give us large quantities of it, some was for us and some was to sell. She was also a schoolteacher but selling Meth was basically a side hustle for her.

Somewhere along the way I suspected people at work found out what I was up to, because they kept coming by to see if I was ok, and one co-worker called me to tell me she had a dream I had relapsed. Clearly, one of the clients I was seeing at the dealers house must have told her. Not that I don't believe in dreams being premonitions, I of all people know that can happen. But in this situation it only made sense that seeing a counselor at the dealers house would be a hot topic at the DUI school. Eventually, that co-worker showed up at my place with my former counselor Beth, in an attempt to conduct an intervention. I denied that anything was amiss and sent them away.

Justin began disappearing for hours at a time. It didn't take long to figure out he was out there committing the same crimes that got him into prison in the first place, breaking into countless parked cars. Pretty much every Meth user has a something that they like to focus on when they are high, the slang term for this is "tweak on." My first go round with the needle, poking holes in myself to find a vein was my "tweak." Justin's tweak was, breaking into cars and occasional houses. He also liked to collect items from the cars, usually wallets with drivers licenses and he was rapidly collecting a plethora of those.

I was sliding back into my tweak of poking holes but this time around I had a conscience about it, due to the fact that I had had a spiritual awakening. I have to say, using with a conscience about it is a very haunting experience. You know what you're doing is wrong and have to make a daily choice to stay on that wrong path. I was in a constant spiritual battle with myself and one night I accidentally injected bleach.

I realized what I had done, when the sudden smell of bleach flooded my senses and I realized the dried up crystallized substance I scraped off of the mirror must have actually been bleach. Shortly afterwards the painful sensation of millions of needle pricks all over my body, all at once, began. I could only assume were my nerves.

I was miserable and out of control. Justin was out of control. My life, our lives were a total catastrophe. Oh, and the most important person in the room. My baby. I thought I was going to die. All I could do is stare at him as I wondered why in the hell I destroyed everything by using again. Why did I do that to him? He was the most special person in the entire world, the best thing that ever happened to me, I had my shit together then I threw it all away at a time when my life was the best it had ever been.

What would happen if I died?

Would my son grow up never even knowing me?

Or would he know the story and wonder what kind of mother would do that to her son?

It was time to stop screwing around with my life, with my son's life, with all of the self destruction, *God, I am sorry for what I have done and I hope you will forgive me and help me correct this situation before it's too late,* I prayed.

"We need to quit doing all of this shit and focus on the baby before something happens and we can't" I said to Justin.

"I am enjoying myself and I don't want to" he replied.

"You need to stop doing all that shit you are doing before the police come and arrest your ass" I shouted.

"Ok" he said as he walked to the door.

"Where are you going?" I prodded.

"I just gotta run out to the car for something" he said.

"You better not be taking off, cause we will not be here waiting for you when you get back" I said to him as I got up and walked over to the door "I called a friend and she said we could go to her house to detox" I told him.

"Ok, we'll talk about it in a minute" he said.

I waited and waited but he did not come back. I went outside and saw that the car was gone, of course. I packed my bags and planned to leave but hesitated. At the end of the night, having given up on Justin, I finally grabbed my bags to leave and as I was walking out I was swarmed by undercover police officers.

He had done what he had been doing and was caught. So he'd been sitting in jail most of the day and they were there to search the place, they had a warrant. I was to a point that I had given up, knowing I was fighting the inevitable so I fully cooperated with them.

As I was being questioned about Justin's behaviors, they searched the place. The only drugs on-site were in my bra, so I wasn't worried about them finding that. They did, however, find the stash of hypodermic needles as well as other paraphernalia so that's when they started in with their questions about drugs.

I openly admitted to being in the midst of a relapse and expressed that I was on my way to a fellow counselor's house to get clean again when they showed up. They asked to look at my arms, I was embarrassed that when I pulled back my sleeves to show them, I had a long trail of dried blood running down the back of my arm. I had no idea the injection site was still bleeding. What a humiliating mess I was.

I began to realize that I wasn't getting out of this one without some jail time, I knew I had a bag of dope in my bra, I asked for permission to use the bathroom. My intention was to flush the eight ball down the toilet.

Due to how cooperative I had been, the investigator did allow me to use the bathroom alone. I pulled the baggie out of my bra with the intention of flushing it down the toilet, but I hesitated. You see I felt like this whole situation was the answer to my prayer for help getting clean again. I suspected if I let them catch me with the drugs, they would give me what I would call a *court assisted* intervention, whereas if I flushed it they might let me off with a slap on the wrist.

I was sleep deprived and under a lot of stress. I was exhausted, I had utterly given up and was accepting of my total defeat in the situation – otherwise I may have flushed it and sought help with one of the hundreds of counselors I knew. I put the baggie back into my bra and went back to the living room. It was at that time the investigator officially informed me he would be arresting me, which he and I, already knew was coming.

I waited until booking, then when I stripped down for the search I handed it to the officer. I was booked into the county jail for Receiving Stolen Property, Possession of Paraphernalia, and Child Endangerment. My six-month-old son was taken into Child Protective Services (CPS).

Six months. That's how old he was when they took him. Considering he was still in the hospital for a while after he was born that means it only took roughly three - four short months to lose literally everything that I built in five years of recovery.

My son. My first and only child. Gone into foster care. Most of my physical belongings were stolen by tweakers including my 1977 Camaro. all of my keepsakes, the respect of the tenants in the apartment complex, the respect of the property management company that I worked for, and of course Justin was likely to get life in Prison under the three strikes law.

I was arrested on a Friday night, which meant a weekend in jail while waiting for court Monday morning, at which time they referred to my son as my *victim* and put a restraining order in place that stated I was not allowed within so many yards of my *victim* without supervision. They released me on my own recognizance with instructions to report to CPS to see my son. Justin wasn't so lucky, they basically wanted to hold him indefinitely, they had no intention of cutting him loose anytime soon.

When I got home I checked the mail and discovered a birthday card from my dad. You know, once again, I think I had forgotten it was my birthday or maybe I was just trying not to think about it since it was on my birthday that the court put a restraining order on me to stay away from my own child, who they said was my victim.

I went home and sat alone in the total mess that I couldn't believe was my house. Grateful that my dad always remembered my birthday, the $50.00 in the card was the only way I would be eating that week.

I was getting calls from Justin's family, he was trying to arrange bail so that he could be with me and attend the visits with our son. It worked out that his parents were able to arrange it.

Once he was home we were staying clean and visiting our son. We no longer had a car so it was a very long walk to the visits but it was worth it. Our son was what was important, and we deserved all of the consequences of our actions.

One night while we were relaxing and watching TV there was a knock at the door. It was the Police. They arrested him again, stating that new evidence had been processed. Not new evidence just evidence they hadn't logged yet, so they were arresting him under new charges. In court, they also denied bail due to him committing a new crime while out on bail even though he didn't.

His bail bondsmen and attorney pointed out to the court that he did not commit a new crime, "Anytime new charges are brought while out on bail, it qualifies as a violation of bail, nothing I can do" the Judge stated.

It seemed the justice system had a real bug up its butt about Justin, maybe he had broken into an off duty police officers car, I'm not sure, but it was clear they wanted to lock him away for as long him up and throw away the key.

I was really depressed, I knew his goose was cooked. It didn't feel right, it didn't seem fair. At my CPS visit they tested me, so when I got home I decided I wanted to get high. My friend encouraged me to not get high, warned me that sometimes they test back to back. I ignored her and went into the bathroom with a syringe. I put the needle into my vein, pulled back the plunger, and just as I was about to inject I thought of my baby.

My son was so young that he was on a fast track for adoption if I screwed up, at all. They had warned me about it already, they don't like to leave a six-month-old baby without stability for very long. Meaning that if a parent struggles with staying clean they'll lose their child pretty fast. I played the tape through and realized the potential consequences of my actions were too severe to take the risk.

That right there, is where my years of recovery saved my life and the relationship with my son. Because I pulled the needle out, threw the drugs away, and the next day my CPS worker sent me for another drug test.

It was an eye opener. My life as a drug user was over. My life as a mother, a responsible parent had just begun.

At one-point Justin's mother came down to attend the CPS visit with my son. We walked into my house afterwards and I couldn't turn on the lights. I was all over that place trying to figure out what was wrong with the lights "Has the power been shut off?" she asked.

Suddenly I couldn't remember when the last time was that I paid the power bill. I was in shock, disbelief and pretty embarrassed. She felt awkward too, I could tell.

The next day I got the three day to pay or quit eviction notice – I was also embarrassed about that. I finally broke down and called my mother. I confessed to everything that had happened and told her I was in trouble.

"We have helped all of the other kids when they needed it, and now it's your turn. How much do you need?" she said.

I told her the cost of the U-Haul, storage, and other expenses and they wired me the money right away. I cleaned the place up as best as I could with no electricity and got myself out of there within the three days to go live with a friend temporarily.

My son had been placed with a really nice, same sex couple of ladies that were looking to adopt. As Christmas rolled around they were trying to keep him to show off to their family but I went to my lawyer and got a court order to have him for Christmas. My CPS worker was quite perturbed with me as we all met up after court "She got herself a court order to keep him for Christmas!" she shouted to the Foster mother.

The Foster mother looked down at the floor, sadly.

"But that doesn't mean I have to follow the court order" the CPS worker said, as she looked at me snidely.

"I do not see why it is important for you to introduce my child to all of your family when he will be coming home with me sooner than you think" I said to her.

"I propose a compromise" my CPS worker said.

"Ok" I said.

"Ok" the Foster mom said.

"You" she pointed at me "Have him for Christmas Eve, then you let them take him on Christmas afternoon, fair?" she said.

"Yes, that's fine" I said. I mean, I got a court order for the entire holiday but she was planning on violating that so I felt a compromise was the only way I'd get to see him at all.

I walked away from that one nervous that my CPS worker would have an issue with me for what I had done. Instead, as soon as the holiday was over, I was given 80% custody of my son for one month, then as soon as I secured a new apartment and had a move in date the Foster moms were instructed to bring me all of his things.

My CPS worker visited the house and told me "What you did is the kind of stuff we are looking for in reunification. You fought for him; you even got a court order. I wish more of my parents were like you."

When the Foster mom came to deliver all of his stuff she was really upset, crying as she said to me, "I don't understand how you got off so lucky."

"I did everything they asked" I told her.

"But they normally throw the book at people! Here you are getting your son back after like no time at all!" she shouted at me.

"This is not my first time in recovery, I was a substance abuse counselor before all of this happened" I told her.

"Well, good luck and treat him better cause he deserves it, and I would have adopted him and given him a better home" she said.

"Thank you" I said to her as I showed her to the door.

Happily Ever After

Satin skin and applesauce breath.
I will always hold you close to my breast.
The truest love I have ever known.
I waited all of my life for this light to be shown.

My son and I moved into our new apartment, which was about as ghetto as anyone could imagine. It was not my first time here, in fact, it's the exact same apartment complex I moved into when I first got out of treatment, I was right underneath my very first apartment. The complex was full of tweakers and cockroaches. The cockroaches were what bothered me, but the tweakers not so much, because I gave zero shits about ever using again.

I was of course without wheels because of my Camaro having been stolen and the only income I had was Welfare – cash aid and food stamps. I filed my taxes, it was my first time filing with a kid, I was shocked when I got $3,000. It was like the most money I'd had all at once in what seemed like forever.

Around that time the CHP was able to get my Camaro back, sadly it had been ripped to shreds inside, as if people thought there were drugs or money stashed in the seats. The steering wheel was hanging on by wires, the engine was frozen. As much as I hated to, I ended up selling it. The body and wheels were worth some money still. Then I found myself a $500.00 car on Craig's List and got myself a telemarketing job.

Once again it seemed like everything I needed, appeared. It's funny how life works that way when you're not knee deep in drugs. I was really enjoying life as an independent single mother. I was no longer insecure about being able to maintain the responsibilities of independence because now I had someone else I needed to take care of.

We had a pretty simple life, I worked full time and was very content sharing my life with this little bundle of joy that always smelled like applesauce. I worked tirelessly to come up with creative ways to sneak Broccoli into meat loafs and burgers. He always smiled at me so widely when I handed him his food, never aware of my diabolical veggie stashes.

On the weekends I rented movies and went to my twelve step meetings. I had been sentenced to community service in the mail room at the Welfare office where I met knew friends and eventually got to transfer to the Alano club where I reported daily to wash the coffee cups for the AA meetings. It was a simple, but happy life.

It didn't go so well for Justin. It took a very long time for sentencing, and we visited him every week that he was in the county jail while he awaited Jury trial. We did a lot of different things to try and help his situation. He even started a movement within the jail to try and get the court to consider that when deciding his fate.

It took well over a year to get to the Jury trial, and I was unable to be there due to work commitments. The Judge began trial staring at the long line of victims, "I am prepared to sentence you to 80 years to life, we'll see if you can convince me otherwise."

There was also a long line of Deputies in attendance, they all worked with Justin throughout his jail stay and they told the Judge about all of the changes he had made in jail, testifying to the fact that he was a changed man who should be offered Drug Diversion instead of Prison. The Judge advised it was due to the support of the Deputies that he would be sentencing Justin to 20 years instead of the 80 years he was initially considering. 20 years in prison is a very long sentence for petty theft but not when you have two strikes against you.

I felt very guilty for plotting the relapse that led to all of that. He resisted using and I pushed until he caved. I was just under some false idea I could control the situation if we used again, including keeping him out of trouble, and I failed because control is an illusion.

He fought for an appeal that never came. I fought for an amendment to the three strikes law, it almost passed and Governor Schwarzenegger stated he'd take a hard look at it but never did. In time, the reality sank in that he really was gonna be in Prison for our sons entire childhood.

Life was good, and the only thing holding me back was waiting around for a love that was lost to Methamphetamine addiction. I had to make the difficult to decision to move on and start dating again. We never know how long we get to have in life, and I felt that I couldn't spend eighteen years of mine on hold - especially when as far as I knew I may not even get that many years, he may not get that many years, the world may not get that many years.

Thirty

Change

~~~
~~~

...And the day came when the risk to remain closed in a bud, became more painful than the risk it took to blossom.

I eventually did get the call that my mother had died and I set course for home in my little Craig's list car and about halfway there a massive cloud of black smoke began to rise from the hood. I pulled over on the first exit I saw and followed the overpass to what looked like a shop of some sort.

Unfortunately, it was not a shop but they let me park there till I could get some help. I called home and my dad called my step-brother. During the wait I was really stressed out that me and my son would be stuck out there in the middle of nowhere. I did not have any money to even get my car fixed, I was lucky I was even able to spare the gas for the trip.

I sat in the back seat to keep my son company; he was a toddler by this point. He actually climbed on top of my lap and started playing peek a boo, he made me laugh, and I could see in his eyes that was exactly what his goal was.

My stepbrother showed up in a truck and towed us to the nearest auto shop where I had to leave my car for them to figure out what in the hell was wrong with it, then we were on our way home.

"You know, it's crazy that you caught me on time cause I had already started to leave, but then there was a bolt of lightning that struck my driveway so I ran back inside. Just as I got back inside the phone rang that you needed help" he said with a smile on his face.

"Wow" I replied and we quietly drove home to a house that neither of us had stood in, in many years.

My mother's services were beautiful. I spent several days there at home hanging out with my stepsiblings and watched my dad laugh at my son as he laid on the couch discovering these alien artifacts on the ends of his arms. He stared at them with the wonder and amazement kin to a spaceship landing on earth.

Mom looked so beautiful in her coffin, "Wow, she looks so young and beautiful" I whispered to my sister.

"That's cause she was, she was only 63" she said.

Well, I survived her death without any new urges to self destruct and I know it's because my son had become my rock. I'm guessing that prior to having a child I was just so lost in the world that I didn't know who I was and the idea of losing a parent was beyond my ability to comprehend. I truly felt terrified of a day when I could lose my father, or my son.

I felt her watching over me, for years to come. I never really had anything concrete but I had always been open to receive communications from spirits, ever since I was a little girl. One day I sensed her presence and I sensed that she was looking out for me. I also sensed she was doing so as a way to make amends for all of the things that had gone wrong between us, a sort of penance. I believe, that even though we fought a lot, we had a strong and sacred bond.

It may not have looked that way on the exterior, but we always hurt the ones we are closest to the most. Many times in life when we're fighting with people we don't realize it's because of a very sacred bond we share. The more we can come to realize that, the sooner we may be able to turn the fighting into acts of love and kindness towards each other.

Either way, it was after her death and my connection to her spirit that I came to see our relationship for what it was. Yes, I suppose that *technically* there was child abuse, but as an adult looking back I understand it was how she expressed herself and sometimes it was a little on the extreme.

All and all she was a very kind and beautiful woman with a temper but she molded the woman that I ultimately became. Strong, determined, able to push through difficult situations. I think it was my determination to beat her all the time that gave me the fight and grit that has gotten me through so many hard times in life.

I guess what I'm saying is *I am grateful for the pain that got me here and am grateful for the pain that keeps me here.* That's a phrase my friend Lou Drew always used and I sometimes couldn't understand what in the heck he meant.

Thirty-One

A Little Girl Grows Up

E verything we needed to know about life, we learned in Kindergarten, including the rules for being human.

You will be given a body.

Love it, or hate it, it is the only one you're getting, so keep that in mind as you go through your life and take care of it as best as you can.

Share with others and make friends.

Friendship is more important than who gets more cookies.

There is always a "somewhere" that will look better than your "here."

When you have one foot in yesterday, and one foot in tomorrow, you're pissing all over today. Cherish the present and remember that the road to success is lined with many thorns, but there will be beautiful flowers along the way.

Flashing forward a bunch of years, imagine a train ride full of adventure, learning to play guitar, becoming a substance abuse counselor, becoming a program coordinator of the treatment center that saved my life, becoming a film producer and authoring my first book (the 1st edition of what you're reading right now).

I mentioned early on that one of the jobs I got when I set off on my own was for the psychic network hotline. This was something I was sort of introduced to when I met my biological mother, who I heard through half siblings had also passed away several years after my mother did. I felt a strong sense of permanent disconnection when I heard the news of her passing. We did not have any relationship at all but now that she had passed it would be too late to change that in the physical sense.

When I was young, I had visited her and watched her giving tarot card readings to people that came to the apartment. Through the years she also worked for the police in helping them solve cases through her psychic abilities. I myself, had not done all of that but in many, many cases I was able to find people I was looking for just by meditating about them for a little while, then I could get into my car and drive to wherever they were.

I also had what I would call very fertile dreams, especially when I was pregnant, and I did read tarot cards for the psychic network hotline, but I did not promote myself as some professional psychic.

I have dreams that frequently come true. It's not only me, it apparently runs in the family because my son has them too and his dreams do come true as well, but he dreams of more specific things like numbers.

One night I dreamt several of my ancestors came to visit me and then my dad's spirit came too. He was crying and full of regret as he sat on the edge of my bed and hugged me, "I'm sorry" he said through the tears.

"No dad don't be sorry, I am sorry" I said as I hugged him back.

He showed me a safe and gave me a combination, 4-5-63-32, "Safe" he said to me.

Then I transformed into a Wolf and walked him to the other side.

I was really upset all night as I wondered if my dad had just died but it was the middle of the night so I couldn't check. I texted him the next day and grew worried as I waited for a reply. Finally, I got a reply "Died a few days ago, thanks for checking in." Then, "Yes I'm fine."

I wrote the dream down on a calendar and tried to chalk it up to being a dream but also made it a goal to see him more often.

I had another dream; in it I was at his house and he had had a heart attack. I was preparing all of these flowers, tons and tons of flowers. I was a little confused as to why because preparing for a celebration of life was not a responsibility that the family usually trusted in me.

These types of dreams kept happening and every time he did have a procedure that he needed to go the hospital for, I was there. It took a couple of years but the dreams did actually end up coming to pass.

I realized pretty quickly that a lot of it was help from my ancestors, probably mom, definitely grandma, they were all helping me to realize I was running out of time. I think they knew that the devastation of him dying would be unbearable to me, especially if I hadn't spent more time with him to make peace.

At one point I got the call that I needed to hurry to the hospital because he was in cardiac arrest and it may be our last opportunity to see him. I rushed out the door, stopping for a second to pray for more time.

I flew down the freeway to him, it was an hour-long drive and my cell phone had died so I had no way of finding out if he was ok or if anyone else was even there.

When I got there his bed was covered in a white sheet, there were a couple of nurses and a doctor in the room. It reminded me of something my biological mother had told me the one time we had spoken a few years before she died.

"Sweetie, I am so sorry to hear that you lost your father" she said.

"I didn't" I told her.

"Oh really? Because I had a dream of him covered in white and kind of floating in a hospital hallway or room" she said. "So that's why I hired a private investigator to find you, because I wanted to make sure you were going to be ok" she said.

"Oh, well he had a close call but he pulled through" I said.

"Oh sweetheart that's wonderful" she said.

Then a couple of weeks later my dad advised me that my mother had taken out credit cards in his name and was running up thousands of dollars in debt, then not paying any of the bills. She had apparently told the banks that he died and she was his widower. After that I never spoke to her again and completely disregarded everything she said.

Now, here I am, arriving in the hospital and all I see is the dream she described to me. He really did look like he was floating, he was covered in white, I was covered in chills at how accurately she dreamed of this years before it happened.

I gradually made my way in and once I got there I saw his face was not covered, "He had a major cardiac incident and he is sleeping" one of the Nurses said "Who are you?"

"I'm his daughter" I replied.

My dad opened his eyes, looked over at the Nurse, nodded to confirm, then closed his eyes again. My dad was tough, some would call him a tough old bastard. Shortly afterwards the rest of the family showed up.

He pulled through, there were additional hospitals, and surgeries but one night I had been looking at old family photos and I saw a picture of him and mom in Hawaii.

Later that night I saw them there in a dream, he had gone and joined her, they were having a lot of fun. I woke up crying, in fear that I dreamed he would be joining her. He was on the mend though and wasn't considered sick enough to stay in the hospital anymore so I assumed it would be some time still, but the next day I got the call that he had passed away.

I began to sob when I got the call, it was as if time stood still and I heard a female voice say this over and over and over again to me free at last. It was an internal voice, but it was loud, loud enough for me to hear her. I suspected it was my stepmother, I also wondered if it was my grandmother, but it really sounded like my stepmother. It could have even been another ancestor I didn't remember from childhood or my biological mother. I am definitely a channeler but not as in tune as I could be.

I wish I would have gotten down there to see him that day but I knew he was being transferred to a new facility for rehab and I just planned on going to see him at the new facility, had I known that it was coming so quickly I am sure I would have.

I had spent a lot of time with him in the previous month but when this kind of thing happens the first thought is. My father died.

The moment I lost him I realized what a mess I had made. I didn't prioritize mending the fences between us. He had been my rock, my hero, my lifeline throughout my entire life. Every bad thing I was up to, he was still there for me even if it was to scold me.

While planning my father's celebration of life, I had the honor of putting together these beautiful bouquets of flowers as we planned food for 100 people, and I got to create a beautiful slide show.

In doing so I combed through all of the old family photos I could find, and I stumbled across photos of him and my stepmother.

It was a blast from a past to be reminded again of how fricking beautiful she was and it was wonderful to see all of the old photos of my dad, he was a handsome and amazing man.

I am so humbled and grateful that I got to walk my journey here on earth in their company.

Thirty-Two

Free At Last

⸎

*A*n ominous cancer raged within the darkness. *Yesterday's sun that caressed and nurtured life was but a distant memory lost.*

A storm of despair and fear was conceived in fury, as I prepared for the sounds of silence.

The lightning struck as a surgeon's knife.

Destruction was swift and final.

To flesh, and dreams of future life.

Thoughts of rising form the pain and fear were thunderous sounds of silence.

The terror of death subsided in the eye,

Replaced with self-pity and surrender.

An exodus of pride and dreams bread malignant tumors of apathy in the mind,

As I accepted the sounds of silence.

It was easy to forsake confidence.

Then slip into the shadows of the tempest.

Yesterday's dreams became the thoughts of failure as lost ambition poisoned the mind and soul. Despair and pain were born from the sounds of silence.

The light struggled through slowly at first, just enough to reflect some silver in the clouds. As rays of hope melted the indifference

Particles of esteem and self-worth fused together, like a laser attacking the sounds of silence. A vibrant rainbow embraced the passing storm. Powered by the music of children's laughter, supported by love, faith and encouragement. It lights the gateway to the impossible dream.

A challenge is issued to the sounds of silence. Dawn brings a new day, a new life, like ivory swans rising on thermals of promise.

Successes path will be lined with failures thorns, but roses will blossom every few miles.

Victory is certain over the sounds of silence.

Today is a kaleidoscope of love and life, filled with opportunity and rewards of endless vision. I no longer cringe and hide from the pain of silence, the quest for speech once lost is fulfilled. Only a distant memory remains of the sounds of silence (The Sounds of Silence, Jack Henslee).

I was and have always been very heartbroken about the loss of my father, although I realize that death is not the end, it feels like the end. It's the end of having him around for all of the everything that I leaned on him for in my life.

I tried to remember that he was free at last, from the body that was failing him, from the hospital stays, from the shackles of being on earth, but I am not sure the little girl inside of me ever really grew up. In fact, I think the child inside of me was always waiting to see daddy and in each time I saw him she grew up a little more.

The thing is that he and I never had the talk. We never sat down and had a candid talk about the past, about the skeletons in the closet, about how he felt about the distance between us, my running away, my relationship with my stepmother, my years of drug use, my years of homelessness after he threw me out onto my ass.

I mean, I had persevered and come full circle but there was always a large barrier between us that I think could have been torn down if we had had a talk about it all. I had my opportunity in that last bit of time I got with him but I had chosen to not use that last bit of time to talk about the past. It just felt too selfish to use what little bit of precious time we had, dredging up memories. The ONLY thing that mattered in that moment was making sure he knew that I loved him and I already knew he loved me.

So, my father was gone, my stepmother was gone and my biological mother had died as well. I did not have any siblings, there were half siblings and step siblings. I hadn't spoken to any of them in along time.

In the end, it was just me and my son. My dad left me the house. The house I grew up in, the house that so much had happened in, the house I'd been kicked out of so many years before, then returned to throughout my life for the holidays. It was the safest place in the entire world, because HE was always there.

It was truly an honor to be given such a beautiful gift. My son and I moved in so that I could go through everything that needed to be gone through but I had a very difficult time doing so.

I had never felt so lonely in my life. It was not lost on me that by the time I returned home everyone else had died and a part of me felt like being there meant I was now at the end of my own road. The house that I would surely grow old and die in as well.

I suppose it's a good thing because we're talking about a house full of so many memories, the light house of my life, the way home for so many years, but I just wasn't ready to settle down to that magnitude.

I was also having so many dreams of my father returning to his body and me needing to move out because it was still his house. Maybe that was triggered by me sleeping in his bed? I am not sure but night after night I dreamt that he was never really cremated, his body was being hidden from us and he would be returning to it and coming home so I needed to go.

It took me the better part of a year to make my decision and I eventually did move. One of the final things that triggered it was my son telling me he needed to find a place to put away his clothes because his closet and dresser were all full of Grandpa's stuff.

It was in that moment that once again I realized that my son was going through a hard time too. I know he lost his Grandpa too but I was all wrapped up in myself and not really thinking of it that way.

He always referred to it as Grandpa's house, even when we were out doing something, it was never "Ready to go home?" It was always "Ready to go back to Grandpa's?"

It was his words that finally drove me to make the change. I was never certain I was making a smart decision but the day that I walked into my new house felt like Christmas morning. I was light, airy and had a bigger smile than I had had in a long, long time.

I think the decision to close the book on that chapter of my life was the most adult decision I had ever made. Adulting is hard.

Thirty-Three

The Afterlife

⁓⟨᳂⟩⁓

I do believe it's true, that there are roads left in both of our shoes.
But if the silence takes you, then I hope it takes me too.
So brown eyes I'll hold you near, cause you're the only song I want to hear.

A melody softly soaring through my atmosphere (Soul Meets Body, Death Cab for Cutie).

Losing a parent reminds us of our own mortality in a way unlike anything else can. I struggled with depression and the feeling that I wasn't sure I understood what life is about anymore.

Why do we collect all of these material possessions? When we die someone is just gonna have to go through it, keep some, give some away, sell some, throw it out, so why do we bother doing any of this stuff at all?

We're born, we grow up, we go off into the world having been taught that we have to have an education, we have to have a job, we have to strive for a career, we have to collect all of these *things* but why? Who decided that was what the human experience was supposed to be about?

Why are we born into these bodies just to do all of that, running around like a bunch of ants until the day it all ends? Becoming so driven to own stuff that we forget what really matters in life?

It was something I began to wrestle with a lot, then I had the dream.

In it, was a scene from the movie Titanic, it was at the end of the movie, when the old woman threw the diamond into the ocean. Then, she went and laid down. Next, she was her younger self, because she had died and the version of herself that her spirit automatically shifted into, was what she had perceived of her best version of herself.

No physical inhibitions of her old failing body, no wrinkles, and a time in her life when she felt the most confident and the most loved.

She walks into the ballroom and all of the people she was on the Titanic that had died were there waiting for her and they greeted her with an overwhelming round of applause. She then met the man she loved the most, the one that she had had to let go of in order to move forward with her own life.

Then, in rapid flashes I saw all of these moments in life, as if they were a slide show of examples, they were in these little snow globe types of bubbles. I saw Christian Kane and Jensen Ackles, singing together on stage in the TV show Supernatural, then their image went into one of those little snow globe bubbles and floated out into the universe. Once it was out there, it sent these waves of light energy all throughout the world and it was explained to me.

These are the moments we get to take with us when we die. We do these things in life because the love, excitement, the energy of it all goes out into the universe like radio waves and it remains out there.

Life is all about accomplishing as much as you possibly can and when it's all over you join your predecessors and everyone gets to rejoice in the accomplishments you had while you were in your human form.

We all come from the same place and are given a body to try and accomplish as much as we possibly can – it's kind of like a competition, in the sense of a scavenger hunt. Even though you don't take the physical stuff with you when you die, you do get to take all of the energy with you, the energy of your accomplishments.

You don't have to be a celebrity to do this, you are the celebrity in your own life. Touch as many lives as you can in a meaningful way, succeed, chase your dreams, and expect a round of applause when you return home where everyone you love, and everyone who loves you that you forgot about, will be waiting to greet you and share the joy of your life.

Death is not the end, it is the beginning of a new existence, a new life, a resurrection from the mundane into the spiritual, when we get to return home. Our true home, the one that we all came from before we walked in these human vessels. We get to take the love with us and that love is where our immortality lives.

Thirty-Four

Be Still and Know

*T*wo roads diverged in a yellow wood,
  And sorry I could not travel both
  And be one traveler, long I stood
And looked down one as far as I could
To where it bent in the undergrowth;

Then took the other, as just as fair,
  And having perhaps the better claim,
  Because it was grassy and wanted wear;
  Though as for that the passing there
  Had worn them really about the same,

And both that morning equally lay
  In leaves no step had trodden black.
  Oh, I kept the first for another day!
  Yet knowing how way leads on to way,
  I doubted if I should ever come back.

I shall be telling this with a sigh

Somewhere ages and ages hence:
Two roads diverged in a wood, and I—
I took the one less traveled by,
And that has made all the difference
(The Road Not Taken, by Robert Frost).

There's a little voice inside of each and every one of us that knows the difference between right and wrong. Everyone has heard their inner voice at some point in their lives.

We see it in movies when a character has a devil on one shoulder and an angel on the other. Has it ever occurred to you that the little voice you hear might not always be your own?

I want to challenge you to try being still and listening to that inner voice more often. When you lay down at night, try clearing your mind of all of your thoughts from the day.

Imagine yourself on a beach.

You're lying on a sandy beach somewhere, your eyes are closed so you do not see anything, but you are very relaxed as you listen to nothing but the sound of the waves rolling in, maybe even a bird off in the distance.

Be still in this moment as you let your entire body relax.

Allow yourself to float.

Now you are floating just above the sand, void of conscious thought, no care about anything except floating freely and listening to the soothing sounds of the ocean. Eventually, you may hear a voice. Try listening to that voice, write down what you hear.

For it is in giving that we receive, and it is in following our instincts that we walk through the doors of contentment, happiness, and immortality of the spirit.

I find that every time I listen to the inner voice I know exactly which door to walk through, which path to take, who I need to go to for help, and most importantly – whatever the goals are that I have in that moment in my life, I find my path to success when I follow the guidance from within.

God's disciples asked where they should build his house "At the top of a mountain?

God said "No, they'll think to look there."

"Well how about at the bottom of the ocean?"

God said "No, they'll look there too."

"I want you to build my house inside of each and every one of them, they will never think to look there."

Thirty-Five

Miles To Go – Two Fireflies

*E*ach Day a New Beginning
It was the same old situation, day in day out. Being public servant felt a lot like slavery. This is the way my world ends.
My world.
My Life.
Life, in a nutshell.
So many people, so much confusion. Day in day out. Punching time cards, begging for vacation days, scrambling to build a savings, spending thousands of dollars on college to try and gain a life that garners more financial resources than minimum wage.
Lose a little.
Gain a little.
Everything is such an uphill battle.
You never really quite achieve the goal.
By the time I was sworn in as Sheriff I had completely given up, given up the idea of cleaning up anything. Until one day it occurred to me, there was a way to control the drug problem, and boost the economy at the same time.
My numbers would soar, I would be a hero, I couldn't see how that would

be a bad thing at all. So, I did it. I began a partnership with the source, the source of most of the drug distribution in the United States. They had a business model that no one could argue with, running all of the drugs through a pharmacy. Hell, even I couldn't argue with it, that shit was legit.

It was flawless from start to finish, and I honestly saw an improvement in the town. Not just financially, but even in the behavior of a lot of the junkie's around town because the product itself was as clean as the driven snow.

Then June Taylor had to come along.

June, the junkie, I had given so many chances to.

June. Who I had helped over and over and over again.

Her?

It really had to be her?

Her and her buddies who banded together to be pains in my ass.

They ruined everything.

Lives were lost, lives that could have been spared, but those lives were nothing compared to the carnage bestowed upon this town if the Cartel found out that the whole operation was exposed.

I tried to stop her, I did, but as they say, "You win some, you lose some." As I lay here, incapacitated, I have to admit, for the first time in my life, "I lost."

It's the little things in life. Those are the ones that get you and you never see it coming until, boom! Now that it's too late you realize that when it comes to the little things in life, there's really nothing bigger.

About the Author

Shawnda Darice Christiansen struggled with addiction at a young age, then at the age of 25 was admitted into an inpatient residential substance abuse treatment center. After treatment she began college, and in time achieved her AA degree in social sciences. During this time she obtained employment as a counselor in an outpatient DUI school.

After a number of years Christiansen began working at the inpatient treatment center where she was once a resident - initially as the intake worker, but she was soon promoted to counselor, then senior counselor, and eventually became the program coordinator of the facility. During the course of this progress, she also became a Certified Alcoholism and Drug addiction specialist and obtained her Bachelor's degree in Psychology.

After 11 years in the counseling profession Christiansen began to dream of a career that allowed her to be outdoors, maybe even a new city. She regretted leaving the counseling profession, because doing that great work allowed her to give back the miracle of hope that had been so feely given to her, but the idea of telling a story about a Junkie who changes her life gave her the idea that she could still give back - just through a different means. Ultimately she decided to write a series of books and produce a series of films portraying exactly that.

Christiansen has written two books, *JUNKIE: Broken Wings* (available worldwide on many platforms) and *JUNKIE II: FIREFLY* (coming in 2019) Miles To Go On Broken Wings is the 2nd edition of JUNKIE: Broken Wings.

Christiansen has written/produced several films:

JUNKIE (available worldwide).

Six Feet of Separation (a COVID documentary available worldwide).

The Slayer Chronicles, Volume I - releasing worldwide in 2021 and is also writing the series of Slayer Chronicles books that will release in 2021.

Christiansen lives in Sacramento, CA with her only son. (She's also a ghost hunter by night!)

You can connect with me on:

🌐 https://www.megareelentertainment.com

🐦 https://twitter.com/shawndadarice1

📘 https://www.facebook.com/shawndadarice

Also by Shawnda Christiansen

Films and books to add to your weekend entertainment.

JUNKIE

The book you just read is the true story that inspired the film JUNKIE aka Miles To Go. Starring Anna Easteden, Eve Mauro, James Duval, and Christian Kane. Directed by Tim Russ.

Available Now.

Six Feet Of Separation

Millions forced into solitude for months, grapple with loneliness and the fear of losing everything they have. Featuring Dee Wallace and Kevin Sorbo.

Available Now.

The Slayer Chronicles - Volume I

Raven Cross walks in two worlds, the mundane and the spiritual; as she solves mysteries of a paranormal variety.

VOLUME I: A nest of vampires uses social media to catch some dinner.

Look for this novel in 2021.

The Slayer Chronicles - Volume I

A nest of vampires uses social media to catch some dinner, starring Madison Russ and Richard Tyson. Premiering in 2021.

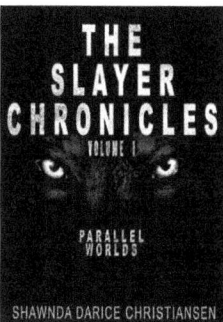

The Slayer Chronicles - Parallel Worlds

A short story introducing Raven Cross, read it free today on Amazon while you await the novel.